THE
PRINCIPLES OF EXPRESSION
IN PIANOFORTE PLAYING

by

Adloph F. Christiani

DA CAPO PRESS • NEW YORK • 1974

Library of Congress Cataloging in Publication Data

Christiani, Adolph Friedrich, 1836-1885.
  The principles of expression in pianoforte playing.

  (Da Capo Press music reprint series)
  Reprint of the ed. published by Harper, New York.
  1. Piano music—Interpretation (Phrasing, dynamics,
etc.) I. Title.
MT235.C55   1974   786.3'04'1   74-1348
ISBN 0-306-70623-7

Published by Da Capo Press, Inc.
A Subsidiary of Plenum Publishing Corporation
227 West 17th Street, New York, N.Y. 10011

THE

PRINCIPLES OF EXPRESSION

IN PIANOFORTE PLAYING

BY

ADOLPH F. CHRISTIANI

NEW YORK

HARPER & BROTHERS, FRANKLIN SQUARE

TO

FRANZ LISZT

THE GREAT MAGICIAN OF THE PIANOFORTE

THIS WORK

IN ADMIRATION OF HIS MATCHLESS GENIUS

AND IN RECOGNITION OF HIS SYMPATHETIC KINDNESS

𝕴𝖘 𝕺𝖚𝖙𝖎𝖋𝖚𝖑𝖑𝖞 𝕴𝖓𝖘𝖈𝖗𝖎𝖇𝖊𝖉

BY A. F. CHRISTIANI

PREFACE.

IN writing this work, I had not only the object in view of providing for those interested in the subject a book of reference, containing a systematic exposition of the principles of expression in pianoforte playing, but I also wished to dispel the erroneous popular belief, that expression is a manifestation of feeling *only*, or that feeling is the sole basis of expression.

I shall endeavor to prove that intelligence, not feeling, is the chief requirement in expression.

Fully twenty years ago, when first the idea dawned upon me, that expression was based upon principles, and not merely upon emotional impulse or individual taste, I asked myself and others: What are those principles? How can I obtain a knowledge, where find a clear exposition of them?

My own teachers had never mentioned the subject, and I venture to say that the conditions of musical teaching, so far as expression goes, are pretty much the same to-day, as they were twenty years ago. Every artist and musician to whom I applied had only private opinions to give on the subject. I searched in German, French, and English literature for more substantial information, but was astonished at the almost total absence of any practical doctrine regarding the laws of expression.

For years I collected every scrap of obtainable information, and, in recording my own deductions, was careful throughout to be guided only by natural laws, avoiding absolutely (as every teacher should do) personal inclination: Sifting and classifying this material, I discovered logical connections between many apparent contradictions, and, gradually, succeeded in systematizing, for my own use in teaching, the leading principles of pianistic expression.

After a test of many years, in which the application of these principles has been most advantageous to myself and my pupils, and thinking that an amplified exposition of them might be useful to others, I determined upon the compilation of this work, which, during the last five years, has filled up the measure of my spare time.

Notwithstanding all the pains I have bestowed upon its preparation, I am fully aware of its numerous imperfections. But, as the higher the aim, the further removed must be the point of excellence aimed at, even as the more we learn, the wider the field of knowledge becomes, disclosing to us the infinitely small share of merit we may claim in any undertaking, I can only trust that this book may benefit those for whom it is written, and leave it to the fair judgment of critics, who, while they find it easy to detect faults, can also duly appreciate difficulties.

ADOLPH F. CHRISTIANI.

NEW YORK, *January,* 1885.

TABLE OF CONTENTS.

INTRODUCTION.

	PAGE
I.—*The Motors of Musical Expression*	11
Emotion and Thought	11
Pianistic Requirements	12
1. Talent	12
2. Emotion	13
3. Intelligence	14
4. Technique	14
Table of Probable Results	16
Subjective and Objective Conception	16
Expression merely an Agent	17
Emotional Expression	18
Intellectual Expression	18
Emotional and Intellectual Expression Combined	19
Which of these Expressions is teachable ?	19
The Mechanical Process of Expression	20
The Mechanical Means of Expression	21
II.—*Accents in General*	22
Their usual Classification	22
Accentus Ecclesiastici	22
How to give Accents	23
Remarks on Touch	24
Sustained Accents	26
Short Accents	27
When and where to give Accents	29
Classification of Accents	31
III.—*Rhythm and Metric*	32
Rhythm defined	32
Historical Sketch of Rhythm	34
Metric defined	42
Metric, the Architectonic of Music	44

PART I.—Rhythmical Accents.

	PAGE
Preliminary Remarks	46
Grammatical Accents	46

CHAPTER I.—*Positive Grammatical Accents* 47

Rhythmic Notation of Eminent Composers	52
Chopin's Notation	53
Hummel's Notation	56
Beethoven's Notation	59
Relation of Grammatical Accents to Time	62

CHAPTER II.—*Negative Grammatical Accents* 69

1. Syncopic Accents	70
2. Removed Accents	74
Phrasing (Metrical, Melodic, Rhythmic)	75
First Phase of Negative Accents	78
Second Phase of Negative Accents	82
Third Phase of Negative Accents	86

CHAPTER III.—*Characteristic Accents* 93

Positive Characteristic Accents	94
Accentuation of the Polka	95
Accentuation of the Polonaise	96
Accentuation of the Bolero	96
Hungarian Music	97
Individual Characteristic Accents	99
Chopin's Accentuation	101

PART II.—Metrical Accents.

Preliminary Remarks	103

CHAPTER IV.—*Metrical Formation. General Facts and Rules* 105

Regular Periods	107
Irregular Periods	110
Examples of Regular and Irregular Periods	113

PART III.—Melodic Accents.

General Observations	138

CHAPTER V.—*Thematic Accents* 141

Thematic Transformations	146

PAGE

CHAPTER VI.—*Accents of Extremes* 154

CHAPTER VII.—*Accents of Slurs*.. 160

CHAPTER VIII.—*Quantitative Accents*... 171

PART IV.—HARMONIC ACCENTS.

Introductory Remarks.. 180

CHAPTER IX.—*Accents of Dissonances*... 182

CHAPTER X.—*Melodic Dissonances or Accessory Notes*............................. 189

    1. Regular Neighboring Notes.. 190
    2. Irregular Neighboring Notes.. 191
    3. Regular Passing Notes.. 192
    4. Irregular Passing Notes.. 194

CHAPTER XI.—*Harmonic Dissonances*... 196

    Anticipation.. 196
    Retardation (Suspension).. 196
    Unprepared Suspensions.. 200
    Accentuation of Dissonances... 202
    Utility of Dissonances.. 205

CHAPTER XII.—*Modulating Notes*.. 209

    Organ-points.. 215

PART V.—DYNAMICS.

Introductory Remarks.. 218

CHAPTER XIII.—*The Dynamics of Melody*... 221

    Melody Unaccompanied.. 221
    Melody Accompanied.. 222
        a. Plain Melody, with Simple Accompaniment............... 223
        b. Plainly Discernible Melody, with Complicated Accompaniment...... 224
        c. Not Plainly Discernible Melodies............................... 226
        d. Hidden Melodies.. 227
    Short Themes and Motives 232
    Several Melodies together 234
        a. Of Equal Importance.. 234
        b. Of Unequal Importance.. 234

	PAGE
Incidental Melodies	237
The Dynamics of Fundamental Basses	238
The Dynamics of Accompaniments	242
CHAPTER XIV.—*Crescendo and Diminuendo*	243
1. *Crescendo* in Rising, and *Diminuendo* in Falling Motion (Normal)	244
2. *Crescendo* and *Diminuendo* in Rotary Motion (Neutral)	246
3. *Crescendo* toward, and *Diminuendo* from, an Accented Point (Neutral)	249
4. *Crescendo* in Falling, and *Diminuendo* in Rising Motion (Abnormal)	253
a. Ascending *Diminuendo*	254
b. Descending *Crescendo*	254
Sudden Dynamic Changes	255

PART VI.—Time.

Introductory Remarks	259
CHAPTER XV.—*Tact and Tempo*	259
Degrees of Tempo	261
CHAPTER XVI.—*Accelerando and Ritardando*	264
Remarks and Examples of	
1. Carl Czerny	264
2. Dr. Ad. Kullak	271
3. Mathis Lussy	276
CHAPTER XVII.—*Sudden Changes of Tempo*	296
Tenuto and *Fermate*	298
Rubato	299

INTRODUCTION.

I.—THE MOTORS OF MUSICAL EXPRESSION.

THE popular assertion "Music is the language of the emotions" should not be accepted as though music expressed emotion only; for it expresses thought as well, and sometimes even thought without emotion. But if we admit the above assertion, it is because music is the chief art medium for expressing the emotions; capable not only of commanding, but of communicating them to others.

There are philosophers who affirm that emotion and thought spring from the same source, the soul, and are inseparably connected with each other; while others say "Emotion is weakened by the association of thought, whereas thought is strengthened by emotion." It is, nevertheless, an indisputable necessity that in music both should go together, simply because emotion cannot be expressed without thought, and thought without emotion is too cold and positive to fulfil the art object of music.

Emotions are often so deep and powerful, yet so complex and intangible as to be unable of themselves to find an outlet. Thought must first prepare the way by concentrating them into some definite idea or ideas. These ideas—conceived by emotion and shaped by thought—are not yet the artistic expression of preceding emotions, but simply their first utterances. Full expression is only to be looked for, when thought again has developed these ideas into a complete art form.

This concentrating and arranging power of thought acts on the emotions as filtration acts on turbid liquids, clarifying and purifying them. And what the emotions lose in intensity and fervor by this process, they gain in clearness and homogeneity; whereas, without the association of thought, emotions would either pass away unexpressed, or remain vague and complex, unable to find expression.

"The human mind cannot with impunity surrender itself to the constant domination of any class of emotions, even of the calmest and purest kind. The perpetuity of a single emotion is insanity." If this assertion of Taylor is correct, purely emotional music, if such were possible, would then be the work of a madman, and of course of no value. Hence, purely emotional music is not to be thought of.

But there is such a thing as purely intellectual music; for instance, strictly constructed canons and fugues, which are essentially scientific works, void of fantasy and spontaneity, more the product of calculation than of inspiration, and frequently written with a total absence of emotion. This kind of music, though appealing to the mind only, is yet of great significance in musical art, not merely as historical form (still accessorily employed in masses, oratorios, etc.), but as instructive form, indispensable to scholarly training.

It is evident that the art object of music is to appeal to the heart as well as to the mind, to portray emotions clothed in musical thought, and to express musical thoughts conceived by the emotions. Therefore, in order to be indeed a cosmopolitan language, music must express both emotion and thought. Hence, emotion and thought are intrinsically the motors of musical expression.

Having thus at the outset referred to these motors, I come at once to the interpreter, the musician, who is either a composer or a performer, and sometimes both.

The composer is the primary interpreter, the conceiver of ideas, which he expresses by the means of thought, aided by theoretical knowledge.

The performer is the secondary interpreter, the diviner of another person's ideas, which he reproduces and represents also by the means of thought, aided by technical skill.

Leaving the subject of emotion and thought with reference to the composer, I turn to the executive musician, more especially the pianist.

A pianist, to be an artist, requires certain endowments, qualities and attainments, which for the sake of brevity I class under the following heads:

TALENT; EMOTION; INTELLIGENCE; TECHNIQUE.

1. TALENT implies a peculiar aptitude for a special employment; hence, pianistic talent implies a peculiar aptitude for that particular branch of musical art. Talent depends more on special training and untiring diligence than on intuitive force; for intuitive force is genius.

Musical talent may and may not imply pianistic talent; but, taken separately, the former is of a higher order than the latter. A pianist may be a great specialist without being much of a musician, but to be a truly great artist he should be an accomplished musician also.

The peculiar aptitude which constitutes pianistic talent, consists in the command of certain organs and faculties pertaining to music in general and the pianoforte in particular, such as a musical ear and memory, etc., but more especially in the gift of fine, delicate touch, which I may call *inborn touch*.

Touch, in its vulgar sense, is mechanical, teachable, and belongs to technique; in its nobler sense, it is a gift, unteachable, and belongs to talent, if not to emotion. For, there is a certain *timbre* in inborn touch (as in a voice), an indescribable something, emanating, as it were, from the fibres of the soul, which directly indicates and appeals to emotion. Inborn touch has an inherent power, which, to a certain extent can move and charm the listener, even without brilliant technique. When such a touch has had high training, it becomes the most notable characteristic of the refined artist, and constitutes—owing to its origin—the æsthetical element of artistic technique. But when this gift is wanting, even the best trained technique cannot supply it. Mechanical and intellectual training may be able to refine the quality of ordinary touch and even elevate technique to the standard of the virtuoso; but without the inborn gift of touch, supplying, so to say, the spiritual element, technique would ever lack its highest element of beauty.

Talent being a gift, is not to be acquired by any effort of mind, nor can the greatest perseverance compensate for the want of it. At the same time, without going so far as Buffon, and asserting that "Patience is Genius," it may be conceded that perseverance will lead farther than talent, if talent be indolent.

Talent either exists, or it does not; it rarely slumbers, and if it does not manifest itself when appealed to, it will never awaken. I do not know of any case where talent first appeared in the guise of the ugly duckling and turned afterwards into a beautiful swan, (as in Andersen's fairy tales). Talent is the swan from the outset.

2. In the term EMOTION, I comprise all that warmth and feeling, emanating from the soul, which can neither be analyzed nor imparted; that divine spark, the "*feu sacré*," which is given to some elect natures only; that source of all artistic creation, "fantasy, imagination;" that sixth sense, "the power of conceiving and divining the beautiful," which is the exclusive gift of God to the artist. This power of conceiving and divining the beautiful may in truth be called the æsthetical sense. It involves the germs and instinct of several minor faculties, such as natural taste and instinctive discrimination; these, however, like talent, in order to become perfected, depend on intellectual training. Then, only, does natural taste

become cultured refinement, and instinctive discrimination become sound judgment.

3. The term INTELLIGENCE presupposes capacity, and comprises all musical attainments that are teachable, viz., skill and knowledge; and also all those appreciative qualities required by the intellectual perfection of the above mentioned faculties, elevating them into cultured refinement, good taste, and sound judgment. In fact, it requires each and every musical attainment acquirable by the exercise of thought and mind, including self-control, mastery of emotion, and repose.

Intelligence aids and corrects talent; it guides and regulates emotion, and directs technique.

4. TECHNIQUE is, in a certain sense, the opposite of æsthetics; inasmuch as æsthetics have to do with the perceptions of a work of art, and technique with the embodiment of it.

Pianistic technique implies, in its widest sense, a faultless mastery of every mechanical difficulty in the required tempo, and without any perceptible effort. It supposes correct fingering, (though, as long as the execution is faultless, it matters not to the listener whether an established, correct fingering is used, or an extraordinary, unusual one,) and it requires a precise touch, with the appropriate degrees of strength, and gradations of strength.

Therefore, technique comprises more than mechanism. Mechanism is merely the manual part of technique, not requiring any directing thought; technique, however, requires thought. For example: As to fingering, which precedes mechanism; as to tempo, which governs mechanism; as to force, which qualifies mechanism; as to touch, which ennobles mechanism. Mechanism is, therefore, within technique, and forms the mechanical element of it, as beauty of touch forms the artistic element of technique.

Dr. A. Kullak asks, " Where does mechanism end? Where does technique begin?"

I reply: Mechanism ends where thought is added to it. Technique begins where mechanism has already attained a certain grade of perfection. A child studying five-finger exercises is studying the mechanism of pianoforte playing; only after years of hard work can it attain a certain technique.

Technique should not seek to shine by itself, and least of all give the impression of being the performer's strongest point. It is not so much a question of playing a great many notes with great velocity in a given degree of strength, as to play every note clearly, and in the spirit of the composition.

A certain professor of music, (in Chicago, I believe,) defines technique as "the ability to strike the greatest number of notes in the smallest possible space of time." But, as Köhler very correctly observes: "Even bad pianists can play quickly."

The quality of the true artist is best shown in his rendering of small pieces, for in larger works—as in scenic painting—the finer details, the deeper toning, the artistic touches are either overlooked in, or overshadowed by, technical bombast, which often covers a multitude of sins. There are many public performers who manage to get through a difficult composition of Liszt's who could not play decently a simple nocturne of Field's, because, paradoxical though it may seem, such pieces are too difficult for them.

Technique, being mechanical rather than artistic, does not of itself make the artist, and giving evidence of persevering labor rather than of talent, ranks—*æsthetically speaking*—lowest among pianistic attainments, although it is really the most brilliant of them and absolutely indispensable. But when technique, already faultless, is qualified by refinement and poetry in touch and taste, it ceases to be simply mechanical, and becomes artistic.

Technique is as indispensable to, and dependent on touch, as touch is indispensable to and dependent on technique.

Of these four pianistic requisites let us consider talent to be the first. The remaining three would follow in this order:

EMOTION, representing the æsthetical element, being the highest.
INTELLIGENCE, representing the scientific element, coming next.
TECHNIQUE, representing the mechanical element, the last.

This would be the order viewed from an artistic point, but if viewed from a popular point, strange to say, the reverse is the case; then technique is the highest, intelligence next, emotion last.

Emotion, when present, is little understood by the great public, but when *not* present, every one feels there is something wanting.

Emotions, being the interior, the innermost part of art, are to the public the most remote; technique, being the exterior, the outermost part of art, is the nearest to the public, therefore the easiest understood and most appreciated. But this is the judgment of the multitude. The connoisseur judges otherwise.

I have said it requires talent, emotion, intelligence and technique to make an artist; what then would be the result if one or more of these four requisites were wanting?

The following table will suggest such probable results :

With				The Highest Obtainable Result would be :
Talent.	Emotion.	Intelligence.	Technique.	
1	2	3	4	Executive artist, of highest order.
1	2	3	..	Non-executive artist ; probably first-class teacher.
1	2	..	4	Natural artist, without musical training ; for instance, Hungarian gypsy musicians.
1	..	3	4	Executant musician ; probably scholarly and critical, but dry.
1	2	..	..	Enthusiastic music-lover ; more impulsive than discriminating.
1	..	3	..	Probably a good teacher.
1	..	..	4	A virtuoso, without being either an artist or a musician.
1	..	..	..	An individual possessing the key to a treasure-chamber, without ever having opened the door.
..	2	3	4	An ever-laboring artist, whose life is too short to attain the perfection he aims at.
..	2	3	..	Artistic connoisseur ; probably a good art-critic.
..	2	..	4	Spasmodic executant ; for instance, certain lady pianists with more sentimentality than judgment.
..	2	..	..	Music-lover by instinct ; a good listener.
..	..	3	4	Scholarly executant, but cold.
..	..	3	..	Musical theorist.
..	..	..	4	Virtuoso of the music-box kind.

A pianist possessing these four requisites is, of course, capable of conceiving a musical work in the spirit of a master, and of expressing his conception thereof adequately and intelligently.

This he may do in numerous ways. But, although the artistic rendering of a musical work may be different in a thousand ways, yet it is generally more or less either subjective or objective, depending upon whether the executant's emotion or intelligence is the stronger. (This refers, of course, only to the master, for the amateur's conception may be anything.)

In case of emotion being the stronger, the conception will be a *subjective* one. The artist will treat the work as though he himself had composed it, subject to his own feelings.

Such an artist is Rubinstein.

On the other hand, where a performer's intelligence is the stronger, his conception will be an *objective* one. The artist will treat the work exclusively in the spirit and character of the composer, making the composer's ideas the object of his attention.

Such an artist is Von Bülow.

I have not thought it necessary to mention technique in connection with these two great masters, for with them technique is what it ought to be—the means and not the end. But there are pianists with whom technique is by far the most prominent, and not seldom the only strong point. These imagine that technique is not only the most necessary requirement (which cannot be denied), but also the highest (which it certainly is not).

But although the multitude will go into raptures over musical gymnastics, yet, as truly as *piano* playing will win more friends than *forte* playing, so will expression always win the palm over mere technique.

Expression is often called "the soul of music"; so I may as well call technique "the body"; both should always go together. Technique without expression has no charms, and soon becomes tedious, like music produced by a music-box, or an automaton—a body with mechanical appliances inside, but without a soul. On the other hand, expression without the necessary technique is impossible, because unattainable.

Expression has no existence in itself, and is only called into life when there is something to be expressed; hence expression is but an agent or conductor, emotion and intelligence being the motors.

Every performer (excepting the dullard who expresses nothing) has a certain individuality according to which he expresses himself. Such individuality may not apparently differ from some other person's style of playing, which it may even resemble as closely as one leaf resembles another, and yet, as with leaves, so with players, it is impossible to find two exactly alike. But although individual expression, with its countless subtle grades and shades, is as varied as performers are numerous, yet the motors thereof are in all cases the same. Hence I may classify expression, according to its motors, into three kinds:

Where emotion is without intelligence.
Where intelligence is without emotion.
Where emotion and intelligence are combined.

Let us now examine into the nature and effects of each of these, in order to determine which is of the highest order, which is indispensable, and which may be dispensed with. Let us see which of these expressions is teachable, and to what extent, and then let us enumerate and examine the means of expression that are at the disposal of the pianist.

1. Emotional Expression without Intelligence.

Emotional expression, being impulsive and warm rather than thoughtful, comes forth spontaneously on the inspiration of the moment, either in tenderness or passion, in gentle murmuring or wild abandon. Discarding all preconception or planning, it is carried away headlong and heedless of restraint, without taking due notice of either means or detail. Though sometimes beautiful, yet often caricaturing the noblest and deepest feelings, it generally oversteps the limits of moderation and good taste and degenerates into the ludicrous, thus converting into positive defects the very elements of beauty it possesses. Hence, it follows, that left to itself and unguided by intelligence, emotional expression is at its best only the fitful effort of exaggerated sensibility; neither artistic nor scholarly; more often a nuisance than a thing of beauty, and therefore, the least desirable.

Listen to sentimental lady performers overflowing with emotion, or to the nervously sensitive, or to the immature musician imagining himself to be æsthetical. Mark how they proceed by fits and starts; accenting always violently, and generally in the wrong places; torturing you with sudden and uncalled-for changes from fortissimo to pianissimo, with out-of-time playing which they believe to be rubato, and with mostly exaggerated efforts, which, no doubt, spring from their inner feelings, but with which the mind and understanding have nothing to do.

2. Intellectual Expression without Emotion.

Intellectual expression, being calculating and cold rather than impulsive, is essentially scholarly and in all cases indispensable. A purely intellectual performer will analyze a work scrupulously to arrive at a judgment of its distinctive characteristics and to get at the author's meaning. He will then form in his mind a plan, even to the minutest details, and execute the composition according to that plan, without deviating from it.

" Distinct but distant, clear, but oh, how cold! "

This is intellectual expression in the abstract, yet it has its attractive side, which is to be found in the perfection of details, as painting in miniature; in scholarly interpretation, shading, phrasing and accentuation. An intelligent musician, without an atom of emotion, can yet, by these means, make his playing so intellectually expressive and interesting, that though, to use a German distinction, he may not *aufregen*, that is, excite, he may yet *anregen*, that is, animate. It must, at any rate, be conceded that intellectual playing, with the exclusion of the emotional, is greatly preferable to an emotional performance, with the exclusion of the intellectual. Who would not rather listen to an intelligent player without emotion, than to an emotional one without intelligence?

3. Emotional and Intellectual Expression Combined.

But

> "Wo das Strenge mit dem Zarten,
> Wo Starkes sich und Mildes paarten,
> Da giebt es einen guten Klang."—SCHILLER.

When the fire and impulsiveness of emotion are held in check by the restraining and regulating influence of intellect; when the repose and positiveness of the latter are stirred by the spontaneous inspiration of the former, the one supplying what the other lacks, both going hand-in-hand; then this blending of soul and brain, accompanied by faultless technique, results in the highest attainable executive perfection and artistic beauty.

It may now be concluded that this is the only artistic kind of expression, and of the highest order.

"Intellectual expression," though indispensable, is merely scholarly.

"Emotional expression" is spasmodic, and may be dispensed with.

In reference to the question, "Which of these modes of expression is teachable?" it must be remembered that expression is simply the agent of either emotion, or intelligence, or both; that these are the motors on which its very existence depends, and that, unless the motor is teachable, expression thereof cannot be acquired. Emotion cannot be taught, but, as a grain of seed, lacking warmth and moisture, remains an unfruitful seed till the proper agencies are applied which cause it to germinate, so emotion (unlike talent) may slumber in the young musician's breast and burst forth whenever the right chord to the soul is touched. Many outer influences acting on our inner life, may cause the awakening of the soul. For instance: Emulation, ambition, sudden and violent changes, grief, misfortune, and, above all, awakening love. But even should emotion remain latent, intelligence still is accessible. It is therefore intellectual expression only that can be imparted.

The extent to which intellectual expression can be imparted depends on the extent of intellectual capacity; for as far as this capacity reaches, just so far is its expression teachable.

Before enumerating the means of expression which are at the disposal

of the pianist, it may be desirable to demonstrate why these means are
more mechanical and less æsthetical than those at the disposal of other
musicians, notably the vocalist and (to a less degree) the violoncellist, etc.
And also, that the pianist, because his means of expression are chiefly
mechanical, needs more intelligence and is less dependent on emotion
than other musical artists.

The mechanical process of expression is to be found in the literal meaning of the word expression, *i. e.*, "pressing out." As a person expresses his
feelings toward another by a pressure of the hand, so does a musician
express musical feeling by a pressure upon a tone. This tone-pressing,
emphasizing, or accenting, is the *chief means and the basis* of musical
significance. Although in itself mechanical, it becomes beautiful by
modifying the accented tone through intensifying and decreasing it
(*espressivo*), and further, by giving color and warmth to the accented
tone, through throwing into it such tremor, passion, pathos, as will give
unmistakable evidence of emotion, and thus express the feelings of the
artist in the most effective manner.

But the pianist cannot express his feelings in so direct a way. Among
all musical artists, the vocalist is best qualified and most able to fulfill
these conditions. Next would rank the violinist and the 'cellist; last and
least qualified would come the pianist, and for this reason:

While in singing or in violin playing an individual tone can be sustained and modified by crescendo and diminuendo, this power is not
possible on so positive an instrument as the pianoforte. Other instrumentalists may distinguish themselves by the formation and quality of
their tone alone; a pianist can alter little in the tone already made for
him. He is able to *accentuate*, but unable to modify a tone after the tone
has once been struck. Therefore his accents must necessarily remain
more or less mechanical, depending mainly upon refinement and taste in
touch to give them color, warmth and beauty. There is undoubtedly a
marked difference between the touch of one pianist and that of another—
a difference so apparent that a really great pianist may show his superiority in this respect by the striking of even a single note.

Great improvements have been made in the carrying power and quality
of tone in modern instruments, but "the art of singing on the pianoforte"
has not been advanced by recent pianists. Nor has the contrivance of
producing a slight crescendo, by means of using the pedal after a note is
struck, been improved upon. It may then be inferred that mere touch,
however beautiful, or mechanical devices, however skillful, cannot sufficiently modify the quality of tone in even the best of modern pianofortes,

and that we shall have to wait for improvements in pianoforte building as yet undreamed of, before a pianist can attempt to compete—if ever—in tone modification, hence in expression, with a singer or with most instrumentalists.

A vocalist has still greater facilities. A great diva, though possessing little intelligence, may, principally by this tone-modifying power, affect others with deeper emotion than she herself feels. And when gifted with emotion she may, in addition, throw such pathos and passion into her voice as will carry away her audience. She may accomplish this by the simplest of means, by a little ballad, if only her voice is sweet and true, and the accents of her delivery are tempered by unfeigned and unexaggerated feeling.

A pianist may also at times carry away his audience, but can only accomplish such results under conditional circumstances and by the highest artistic means. He must be a very superior executant, endowed with rare intelligence and talent. He needs a first-class instrument, and a small salon rather than a large hall; and, above all, an audience not only musically educated, but especially interested in pianoforte playing. Without the latter condition the results of even the best pianistic efforts are often more those of admiration and wonder than of sympathy and emotion, such as a far less intellectual vocalist can call forth.

And yet, although the vocalist possesses much greater advantages and facilities, what living singer or instrumentalist is there who is able to enchain and hold an audience of intellectual and cultured people spellbound during the two hours' programme of an unaided pianoforte recital, rendered by a Rubinstein?

It appears then, that the intellectual efforts of a vocalist are not necessarily so great as those of a pianist, while at the same time the results of a vocalist's emotional efforts are far greater. That a vocalist (next to a good voice) most needs emotion, and is less dependent on intelligence, in the same proportion as a pianist most needs intelligence, and is less dependent on emotion. And, while a vocalist may be great without being very intellectual, a pianist cannot be a great artist without being intellectually a superior person.

Having thus shown under what disadvantage the pianist labors with regard to expression, I now enumerate the mechanical means of expression. These are: ACCENTS; DYNAMICS; TIME.

Each of these means will be subjected to careful examination, from which will result an exposition of the principles which naturally govern expression.

II.—ACCENTS IN GENERAL.

IT has been said with truth, " Upon accents the spirit of music depends, because without them there can be no expression." " Without them, there is no more melody in song than in the humming of a bee." Accents hold certainly a far more prominent place in pianoforte playing than is generally accorded to them, and it is to be regretted that they are not made the subject of more careful study.

Theorists mention a confusing variety of accents, most of which, though differing in name, are really identical; but they generally agree in classifying them into two kinds, viz., regular and irregular.

REGULAR ACCENTS.	IRREGULAR ACCENTS.
Grammatical,	Rhetorical,
Measure,	Æsthetical,
Rhythmical,	Emotional,
Metrical,	Descriptive,
Syntactic,	Declamatory,
Syncopic,	Pathetic,
Removed (verschobene),	Oratorical, etc.
Characteristic, etc.	

The character and function of each of these will be mentioned hereafter.

An entirely different meaning from the above modern accents have the old ecclesiastical ones, which depended on, and were subject to, the prosody of words, and formed the only relief in the monotony of Gregorian chants. These, although out of place here, may yet be mentioned to give this enumeration greater completeness.

ACCENTUS ECCLESIASTICI.

This appellation was given to the different formulas for intoning the Epistles, Gospels, Collects, etc., of the Catholic Church service. The intoning, or chanting, was generally delivered in monotones of equal duration, and the "Accentus" consisted of certain inflections at the end of a period, which period depended upon the character of the words, the quantity of syllables, and upon interpunction.

J. G. Walther, in his " Musical Lexicon, Leipzig, 1732," distinguishes seven kinds :

The Accentus was,

1, *immutabilis*, when the last syllable of a word neither rose nor fell.

It was, 2, *medius*, when the last syllable fell a third.

It was, 3, *gravis*, when the last syllable fell a fourth.

It was, 4, *acutus*, when one or more syllables before the last one were intoned a third lower, but the last syllable returned to the principal tone.

It was, 5, *moderatus*, when one or more syllables before the last were intoned a second higher, while the last syllable returned to the principal tone.

It was, 6, *interrogatus*, when in phrases of interrogation the last syllable was intoned a second higher.

It was, 7, *finalis*, when the cantus at the end of a part descended gradually, during the last syllables, a fourth.

The general idea of classifying the before-mentioned accents (leaving the ecclesiastical ones totally aside) into regular and irregular is, that the former are prescribed by the laws of rhythm, and the latter, being dependent on the emotions, cannot be prescribed or indicated by any definite rule.

Theorists say that the irregular accents (emotional, æsthetical, rhetorical, or whatever name may be given to them) have their root in the mood of the performer, and that can neither be anticipated nor dictated. Moreover, lacking the appropriate musical indications for the emotions, a composer cannot indicate them, hence the performer ought to divine them and accent accordingly, although the accents are not indicated. But this is only avoiding a difficulty without trying to substitute a remedy for it. This may be sufficient for the artist or the master, but is quite inadequate for the majority of students and for teaching purposes. Did it never occur to the theorists that there need be no irregular accents at all?

What is the use of writing volumes on musical emotion, and then being obliged to confess that no rules can be laid down for its expression? Would it not be far better to leave the emotions alone, and endeavor to regulate accentuation on a possible and intellectual basis?

Inasmuch, then, as a comprehensible and intellectual theory of accentuation does not as yet exist, most players are guided by instinct and feeling rather than by knowledge and reason. Hence accents are too often overlooked, misplaced, or exaggerated, and the questions arise, *How, when, where and why to give them?*

HOW TO GIVE ACCENTS.

The "how to accent," like everything in pianoforte playing, requires technique, intelligence, and emotion; but is essentially a question of touch, because, whatever intelligence and feeling suggest, is transmitted through the touch.

As a question of touch, it is explainable only so far as touch itself is explainable, and touch can only be explained apart from its emotional elements. I may therefore state that the above question cannot be answered under its emotional aspect, but can be answered under its mechanical and intellectual aspects. Fortunately, technique and intelligence are the essential elements of accentuation, more particularly in pianoforte playing; and feeling, although the beautifying, is not the absolutely necessary element.

I may further state that the emotional part of "how to give accents" is the only thing unteachable in the entire subject of accents and accentuation, and that all else connected with accents, viz.: when, where and why to give them, can be reduced to a comprehensible system.

Returning, now, to the explainable part of how to accent, I approach the subject of touch, in its especial bearing upon accents.

The chief object of touch is to produce tone. Not that kind of tone which anyone can draw from a pianoforte by sinking a key, but a tone perfect in all its requirements. These requirements are:

1. *Purity and clearness of tone.*
    These belong to the mechanical part of touch, which is explained in the general technique of pianoforte playing.

2. *Beauty and expressiveness of tone.*
    These belong to the emotional part—the æsthetical, the indescribable.

3. *Correctness of tone.*
    In respect to force (dynamical),
    In respect to duration (rhythmical).
    This belongs to the intellectual part of touch.

With this we have especially to do.

The purely mechanical part of touch consists in a preparatory finger raising, and the down stroke of the finger—the touch proper.

But this down stroke, or "Anschlag," as the Germans call it, must not be taken literally, as though the key were to be struck; for, where expression is required, it should not be struck. Expression requires pressure—finger pressure. Touch without pressure can never produce either depth of tone or emphasis. Emphasis is pressure.

Through finger pressure arises what the Germans call "Die Tonbildung des Anschlags"—the tone-formation of touch.

Through finger pressure the touch receives its proper degree of force, its duration, its expression.

A special finger pressure, or stress upon a particular tone, produces the accent.

The (degree of) force of accent constitutes its *quality;* the duration its *quantity.*

Thus, quality is dynamical; quantity is rhythmical.

FIRST GENERAL RULE OF ACCENTS.

The quality of accents should not surpass the unaccented notes by more than one degree of strength.

In pianissimo the accent should not exceed piano.				
In piano	"	"	"	mezzoforte.
In mezzoforte	"	"	"	forte.
In forte	"	"	"	fortissimo.

And in fortissimo playing there should still be left enough of reserve strength for accentuation.

The *quality,* or force of stress, has nothing to do with the *quantity* of accents.

The *quantity* of accents depends upon the stress being sustained or not sustained.

If the stress is sustained and (where the instrument permits) modified by swelling (*cres. dim.*), and that indescribable tremor which must be felt to be expressed; then this may be truly called the *expressive accent,* because it is the truest and most direct transmitter of emotion, the nucleus of musical expression, upon which expression chiefly depends. In the usual practice of teaching, such an accent is classed among the irregular ones, and variously called: "rhetorical," "æsthetical," "emotional," "pathetic," etc. The name matters little. (See previous enumeration.) But, as we are here examining the explainable part of accents only, and an expressive accent, as above described, is altogether impossible in pianoforte playing, we will call this simply *sustained accent.*

If, on the other hand, the stress is not sustained, but shortened or cut off, we call this *short accent.*

SECOND GENERAL RULE OF ACCENTS.

The *quantity* of accents is of two and opposite kinds.

Every accent is necessarily either:

1. A *sustained accent.* The idea being a swelling of strength—a pressing out of tone—symbolized thus $\prec$ (see Dynamics), or it is:

2. A *short accent*. The idea being a sudden decrease of force—a shortening of tone.   Symbolized thus $\succ$ (see Dynamics).

A *sustained accent* may be likened to a grasp of the hand, which, now
strong and passionate, now gentle and loving, is always expressive of the
giver's mind and feeling.   Just so with this accent, which is expressive by
its pressure.

Regarding the touch, it is to be observed that in the action of coming
down upon the key there is a momentary feeling of the ivories, and the
touch is like a pressure seeking to exhaust the depth of the keys.

This tone pressure may be given by finger touch, by wrist touch, by
arm touch, or by a combination of these.

Starting from the principle that the higher the finger is raised the
weightier is the touch, it will be perceived that finger touch is the least
weighty, because the finger can only be raised as high as it is long.

If the strength of finger touch does not afford the desired emphasis,
wrist touch is resorted to.

If wrist touch is not emphatic enough, arm, or even shoulder touch, or
a combination of all these touches, may be employed as the occasion requires.

But whether the action of striking the keys comes from the fingers,
from the wrist, from the elbow, or the shoulder, the weight of the touch is
in all cases to be concentrated in the finger points.   Hence arises the
necessity of tightening the wrist at the moment of accenting, because the
wrist, when firm, lends resistance to the finger pressure, and transmits
the weight coming from the arm or shoulder which would otherwise be
lost.

It is essentially a *free-arm touch* (by which is to be understood a combination of finger, hand, and freely raised arm), which is most appropriate
and effective for all purposes of accentuation.

The force of such a free-arm touch can be made to equal almost the
weight of the player, and yet is capable of the nicest gradations.   It can
be given with little or no effort, and its mere weight produces 'a far
nobler tone than could any muscular force.

In reference to the nicety of gradation this kind of touch is capable of,
it may be worth mentioning that in a *Cantilene*, when applied to certain
opening notes, as, for example, to the first note in the melody of Chopin's
"Berceuse," or Döhler's "Nocturne," etc., such a free-arm touch coming

from high above the keys is of beautiful effect, and can be made to produce a more refined tone than if the arm had not been raised.

Short accents, like sustained ones, range through every grade of
strength, and through every phase of emotion.

The touch is the same as in sustained accents, with this difference,
however; whereas, in the latter the power of the tone is supposed to increase, in short accents the pressure instantaneously decreases, the tone
being, so to say, cut off.

Theoretically, relaxation of finger pressure is all that is needed to make
the tone short; for, without raising or withdrawing the finger, without
even quitting the ivories, relaxation of pressure alone is able to cause the
dampers to fall back on the strings. Hence, any subsequent action of
getting the finger away by withdrawing or lifting it, would come after
the tone is already cut off, and would have no effect in making it still
shorter.

But in the actual practice of pianoforte playing, simple relaxation of
finger pressure does not prepare the next coming touch, and as such preparation is almost always necessary, relaxation is accompanied by finger
contraction, by hand raising, or by both, with even additional arm raising.

The shortness, or the staccato so produced, is called " the positive staccato," in opposition to " the negative staccato," which does not require a
preparatory hand or finger raising for the next touch.

The *positive staccato* is practised either in the manner of Hummel, by
contracting the finger almost simultaneously with striking the key, so that
"touch and go" are really one action. Or, by letting, in addition, the
hand rebound upward simultaneously with finger contraction. This re-
bounding demands a very light hand and loose wrist, and gives to the
touch a certain elastic spring which, though it cannot make the tone any
shorter, yet prepares the next coming touch.

The *negative staccato* requires simply a pressure, not a stroke ; a preparatory hand raising is therefore not necessary. The hand is brought in
contact with the keys, the keys are pressed down and the pressure is instantaneously relaxed, with just a sufficient rebound to allow the dampers
to fall back on the strings and the fingers to be prepared for the next
pressure. But there is no raising of the hand from the wrist, the ivories
being hardly quitted by the finger points.

This is not only the shortest, but the most graceful staccato, and applicable to every grade of strength and every shade of delicacy.

BEETHOVEN—Sonata, Op. 14.

The great adaptability of this negative staccato is seen in its fitness for *portamento* purposes (also called *half staccato*), for example in cases like this:

CHOPIN—Impromptu.

When the joining effect of *pedale* is added to this manner of touch, it produces even an almost legato effect.

CHOPIN—Berceuse.

The special employment of negative staccato in reference to accents will be shown hereafter.

Before concluding these few remarks about touch, the following distinctions, implying a logical principle, are worth observing:

The raising of the hand precedes the touch in order to prepare it, and does not follow the touch to make it short.

Shortness depends on the relaxation of pressure on the accented tone, and not on the throwing up of the hands.

I cannot refrain from a warning regarding the throwing up of the hands, a mannerism of many pianists, which does not assist in rendering their short accents any shorter, even if they were to throw up their hands to the ceiling, but lays them open to censure for affectation and artificiality.

Many of even the best teachers dwell too much on the subject of hand-raising, to the neglect of the more important subject of tone-producing.

The constant correcting and admonishing with regard to hand-raising —a thing as self-evident and necessary as the raising of one's foot in order to be able to walk—leads almost always to more faults, than if the subject had only been lightly touched upon, or let alone altogether. Does it follow, because hand-raising is indispensable in octave and other cases of wrist playing, that at every staccato note the pupil should be told to touch the keys as though they were of red-hot iron, and be made afraid to press down a key lest the hand might not get up quickly enough? Trying to obtain shortness of tone at the expense of its quality, by neglecting the necessary pressure which even the shortest accent requires, is like running after a shadow and leaving the substance behind.

While the question "How to give accents" was, under its emotional aspect, inexplicable, permitting but of two general rules, the next question, containing virtually everything else pertaining to musical accentuation, is simply intellectual, and permits of precise rules. I am referring here to accentuation at large, and not merely to rhythmic-metrical accents, which have always been regular and teachable.

WHEN AND WHERE TO GIVE ACCENTS.

To answer this completely and comprehensively is equivalent to reducing musical accentuation to rule. This has always been declared impossible, owing to the indefinable in accentuation contained in the "how," where the emotions come into play.

But when this inexplicable part is excluded, and only the "when" and "where" are considered, it is then possible to reduce accentuation to rule.

Why, then, has not this question been answered before?

Strange as it may seem, there is no evidence in the theoretical musical literature of Germany, England, and France to show that the question when and where to accent, separated from the "how," as applied to musical accentuation at large, has ever suggested itself to the few writers on this subtle subject, far less has it ever been brought forward or investigated.

In the general practice of pianoforte playing the student is referred to the composer's written indications, and, when these indications are insufficient or altogether wanting, the student is thrown on his own resources, but, not knowing the principles of accentuation, accents at hazard, and is almost certain to do so incorrectly. The teacher may suggest some missing accents, or check others that were uncalled for, but the student is seldom told the *reason* or the *principle* according to which these corrections or suggestions were made.

These conditions of *laissez aller*, or find-out-for-yourself, continue until the intelligent student becomes, through long practice, in some measure familiar with the leading principles of accentuation. The knowledge thus acquired rather by discovery than by reasoning is, however, rarely thorough. Individual fancy is almost certain to assume by degrees the place of discrimination, and sooner or later accentuation is allowed to be governed altogether by emotional impulses. To follow the latter might be permissible in deciding " how " to accent, but emotional impulses are the worst of guides in the choice of " when " and " where " to accent.

These are some of the results of the usual system, or, rather, the non-system of letting the student find out for himself when and where to accent.

As no systematic method of accentuation as yet exists, it is high time that an attempt should be made to supply this desideratum.

The few and not very serious efforts which have been made to systematize accentuation could not help failing, because the fact that the inexplicable was not separated from the explainable, made it from the outset impossible to arrive at a satisfactory result. This fundamental mistake led to another, an erroneous and unsatisfactory classification, which in itself alone would have caused failure.

If, then, the present attempt is undertaken in the expectation of better success, this expectation is based on the belief that the primary causes of previous failures have been removed, and because the attempt is limited to the explainable in accentuation.

I hope to bring order and system into the many and often confusing opinions regarding accents, not by any new method conflicting with natural principles, but simply by establishing a logical connection between the natural laws of musical accentuation, and by bringing these laws into a comprehensible whole.

I am aware that, in a great measure, I am entering upon untrodden ground, and I approach the subject with all due diffidence. Should I fail in the attempt, I trust I may at least have traced out a system capable of further development at the hands of one more competent.

As a matter of course, accents should be given only when and where they are required.

To determine this, depends upon knowledge and mature judgment, and not upon individual fancy or emotional impulses.

Accents are always required for the purpose of bringing out and explaining certain points. These points can only belong to one of the four elements constituting the component parts of music, viz. :

RHYTHM ; METRIC ;* MELODY ; HARMONY.

Each element requires at a certain instant of time (the when), and upon some precise spot (the where), an accent. This accent is necessary to make prominent and explain some especial point or principle of the element.

Accents should consequently be classed according to the element which calls for them.

Therefore, as a first step, I commence by classifying accents into as many kinds as music has component parts :

| RHYTHMICAL ACCENTS ; | MELODIC ACCENTS ; |
| METRICAL ACCENTS ; | HARMONIC ACCENTS. |

In the subsequent investigation, each class will be subdivided into a number of different accents belonging to that particular class.

In reference to this classification I have to observe, and it is important to bear this in mind, that of the four component parts of music, rhythm is the element which is everywhere. Every note in a musical composition, every instant of time upon which an accent could fall, is a part or link of rhythm, and, therefore, whenever or wherever an accent is given it is always in a certain sense rhythmical.

And yet, accents are not all rhythmical, because their classification depends more upon the element calling them forth and most affected by them than upon the instant of time they fall on.

Before investigating each one of these four classes of accents, it is quite indispensable to arrive at a clear conception of

What is Rhythm ?

What is Metric ?

---

* The word " Metric " (Germ. *Metrik*) is used in this work throughout as the equiva-lent of "metrical form."

More especially, because many theorists make no distinction between these two elements. Also, because the nature and function of these two elements, and their relation to each other, are, as a rule, very little known or only vaguely understood.

III.—RHYTHM AND METRIC.

"RHYTHM is any motion, especially a regulated, recurring motion;" therefore, "the measure and outline of motion" made clear and comprehensible, as in music, by "the periodical recurrence of accent."

Among the many often suggested similes, rhythm is perhaps best likened to pulsation, and pulsation to rhythm. For rhythm is the pulsation of every kind of movement; and pulsation the rhythm of whatsoever has life.

If pulsation gives the fundamental idea of rhythm, the next idea would be that rhythm is method, for it brings order into every kind of movement.

"It seems to be a necessity for man, if movements of any kind are to be sustained for a length of time"—that, instead of an undivided flow, the movement should be divided into parts, and—"that some more or less strict law of interchange should regulate the succession of these parts. More particularly in order that a number of parts may constitute a whole, or, at all events, a pleasing whole, a certain relation or proportion must be felt to pervade them. When exemplified in the arrangement of matter into visible objects, as in sculpture, architecture, and other plastic arts, rhythm is usually called symmetry."

Symmetry is one of the chief conditions of a work of art, as necessary to one which appeals to the eye as to one which appeals to the ear, as in music and poetry.

Symmetry means "the harmonious proportion of parts to each other, or to the whole." To obtain this harmonious proportion is the object of rhythm in music.

"Rhythm is the principle of order in the magic world of tones. It gives to sound its wavy outlines. It is everywhere, and lends a beautiful self-balance to the out-goings of every unimpeded energy. Every art has its rhythm or something corresponding, and this is why music is so congenial to every form of beauty, and can so readily translate or transfuse the *spirit* of what we feel through other senses than the ear. For rhythm is the law, or common term, uniting all these spheres, and distributing their elements in correspondence with one another."

"Music is chiefly indebted to rhythm for its order, perspicuity, intelligibility, and consequently its power and effect."

Melody and harmony spring directly from the realm of tone,—tone constituting the composer's material, as color constitutes the material of the painter, and words that of the poet.

But a succession of tones alone, without some rhythmical arrangement, would be a doleful monotony, a silly tinkling; as incomprehensible as a mixture of color on a canvas without some perceptible outline; as meaningless as a succession of words without some indwelling sense.

To prevent such incoherence, and to avert monotony, is the principal function of rhythm.

With tones alone, a composer could not express the simplest musical idea, nor the most insignificant melodious phrase, unless he associated with them rhythm, ".that special power which raises the raw material of sound into higher spheres, and makes it an intelligible vehicle of the composer's idea."

Musical rhythm has a double function :

a. QUANTITATIVE, and *b.* QUALITATIVE.

(German theorists call these functions "extensive and intensive.")

a. Rhythm is quantitative, in measuring the quantity (extension) of notes in respect to duration—time.

This is the principle of order which

1. Determines the duration of each tone by giving to every musical sound its rhythmical value, *i. e.,* "the ratio which its duration bears to that of other sounds ;" and

2. Arranges portions of equal rhythmical value in such a way as to fit in, and fill the (metrical) measures, of which a greater or less number make up a musical composition.

b. Rhythm is qualitative, in measuring the quality (intensity) of notes in respect to dynamics, *i. e.,* as to their strength or power.

This is the grammatical principle of rhythm, according to which all rhythmic motion is divided into strong and weak, or accented and unaccented parts.

Thus, if on the one hand rhythm measures quantity (duration), on the other hand it depends on quality (accents) for its logical significance.

The periodical recurrence of accent, formed of the interchange of rising

3

and falling, is necessary to give a clear sense of the rhythm, and lend to the movement its wavy outline.

"This measured beat is like the pulse of life by which we note its movement." And "it is especially this succession of accent and impulses, arranged in alternately advancing and retiring waves, which becomes decisive in the formation of a musical work, and in its reproduction."

HISTORICAL SKETCH OF RHYTHM.

It is generally conceded by musical historians that the earliest manifestation of the principles of rhythm, viz., of measuring and determining motion, must be looked for in the measured step of the march or the dance, whence it was transferred to word and tone.

When word and tone became associated with rhythm, then only was it that poetry and music emerged and joined the sisterhood of the arts.

The beating against each other of any hard or hollow substances, warriors striking their swords against their shields, the use of drums, tambourines, castagnettes, and other percussion instruments, all these produce rhythmical music.

Such primitive music may have been suggested originally by corresponding movements of the body. These rhythmical movements of the body had produced the dance, as the measured step of warriors, or the procession of priests, had produced the march. To better accompany these movements, better musical sounds than loud and jarring noises were discovered in the human voice, and through the invention of musical instruments.

The rhythmical arrangement of these new sounds produced the first real music. Melody, *i. e.*, a pleasing succession of musical sounds, rhythmically arranged, sprang up, and was made to correspond with the already familiar rhythmical movements.

"In the same manner as the rhythmical arrangement of sounds not articulated produced music, the like arrangement of articulated sounds produced the cadences of prose and the measures of verse."

It is not material here to discuss whether rhythm was first employed in the arrangement of articulated sounds (language) or of inarticulated ones (tones), since it is obvious that language existed long before music.

It is sufficient to state, that when music began to be an art, as among the ancient Greeks, the "*Rhythmopoeia*" of the latter (a special science prescribing the laws of rhythm) was solely connected with poetry, and poetry alone regulated the movements of ancient music.

Music and poetry were not only inseparably connected with each other, but together with dancing, gymnastics and dramatic art, they became one art, the art of the Muses.

The principles and entire system of Greek music were, however, so radically opposed to progress; the laws of their musical art so absolutely and despotically prescribed (for example, certain melodies were declared so inviolable that any alteration of them was punished by death), that, as Kiesewetter says in his History of European-Oriental Music, " If old Greece had existed undisturbed for another two thousand years, her music could never have obtained emancipation, or reached the degree of perfection of modern music."

To modern musicians it is now a plain fact, that Greek music was the painfully cultivated, yet ungainly child of mistaken parents, who blindly traced out for it a future entirely opposed to its true mission. We have nothing to regret in its demise, and may thankfully exclaim—" Requiescat in pace ! "

The Romans did nothing for music.

The earliest Christian Church, in its endeavor to purify music from the influences of heathendom, discarded instrumental music altogether and allowed vocal music only.

The next epoch in musical history was that of the Ambrosian chant, from about the fourth to the seventh century.

This was followed by the famous system of the Gregorian chant, from about the seventh to the seventeenth century.

Ambros says (Hist. of Music): " The great vital force of the Gregorian chant strengthened the entire tone art and gave it the right impulse." And Kiesewetter says : " The system left by Gregory and his assistants was in its simplicity so capable of the highest improvements, that a perfect music, like our present, might have been developed out of it, had not the blind preference and veneration of the scholars for the old Greek traditions hindered its development for a long time, by going back to the old theories."

This hindering influence of old traditions asserted itself indeed for a long time; for not until the thirteenth century were the first steps taken towards emancipation, and in the most needed direction, a rhythmical one.

The progress of emancipation lasted until the beginning of the eight-eenth century, when at last, with Bach in Germany, and his great con-temporaries, Händel in England, Rameau in France, A. Scarlatti in Italy, modern music began to bud, to blossom, and gradually to flourish.

Music, until the thirteenth century, meant vocal music; and vocal music meant church or choral music based upon the principles of the Gregorian chant, and practised in unison without harmony.

The Gregorian chant was "movement without measure or time," its mere apology of rhythm (the Accentus Ecclesiastici) was scarcely any rhythm at all; and as it recognized only two rhythmical values, viz., long and short tones, to correspond with the long and short syllables of the words, the general effect, though solemn, was decidedly monotonous.

So long as the Gregorian chant was practised with one voice only (in unison), the old notation of "Neumen" (signs for notes)* was sufficient.

But when polyphonous writing began to develop itself, when (even in the twelfth century) a second voice was added to the tenor—the lead-ing voice in choral music,—then a third, and lastly a fourth voice, each voice having an independent, measured part, it became absolutely necessary to measure accurately the rhythmical value of each tone.

Hence arose the measured (*mensural*) or figured notation as the natu-ral product of this development.

About the beginning of the thirteenth century, the monk Franco, of Cologne, invented the rhythmical division of *four* kinds of notes, by add-ing to the existing short and long notes (Brevis and Longa) a shorter (Semibrevis) and a longer note (Maxima).

---

* *Examples of* NEUMEN.

Ground form, or SIMPLEX NEUMA, viz., Punctus, ■ or ●, as sign for shortness.

Virga, ❘ or ↓ or ➤, as sign for length

Examples of Combinations.

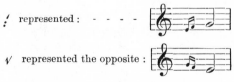

/ represented :   - - - -

√ represented the opposite :

⌇⌇ represented a Tremolo, etc., etc.

These very complicated and numerous signs were first written without lines. Then with one red line for the note F, in the tenor. Next, with a second, yellow line, for the C above. Guido of Arezzo added two uncolored lines, making four in all.

Taking the *brevis* as the unit, the division was this:

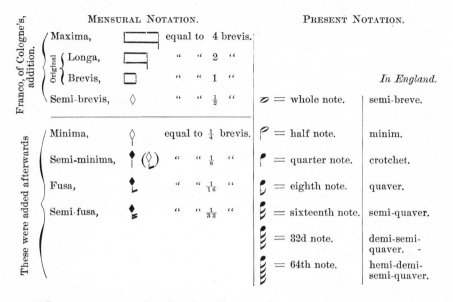

	MENSURAL NOTATION.			PRESENT NOTATION.	
					In England.
Maxima,		equal to	4 brevis.		
Longa,		" "	2 "		
Brevis,		" "	1 "		
Semi-brevis,		" "	½ "	= whole note.	semi-breve.
Minima,		equal to	¼ brevis.	= half note.	minim.
Semi-minima,		" "	⅛ "	= quarter note.	crotchet.
Fusa,		" "	1/16 "	= eighth note.	quaver.
Semi-fusa,		" "	1/32 "	= sixteenth note.	semi-quaver.
				= 32d note.	demi-semi-quaver.
				= 64th note.	hemi-demi-semi-quaver.

Franco, of Cologne's, addition.

Original { Maxima, Longa, Brevis, Semi-brevis

These were added afterwards { Minima, Semi-minima, Fusa, Semi-fusa

"It is a strange fact in the history of music, that every new step towards improvement, whether in the right direction or not, was always and is still met by opposition and indifference.

"Pope John XXII. was indignant at this new invention, which dared to interfere with the established rules of church music, and threatened to destroy melody by cutting the notes into smaller divisions, and by introducing pauses.

"But notwithstanding all opposition, this new invention was so important a step in the right direction, that it could not fail to spread and thrive."

The very intricate and to us most awkward system of *mensural* notation lasted from the thirteenth to the eighteenth century. This latter period, "the early spring time and flowering epoch of musical art," as Bellerman calls it, was the preparatory period of modern music. It was rich in great men and great results, and the lustre of such names as *Okenheim, Willaert, Orlando Lassus,* of the Netherlands school; and *Palestrina, Allegri, Monteverde,* of the Italian school, will shed its radiance on that period forever.

"Owing to the increasing independence of instrumental over vocal music (even in the sixteenth century), additional divisions in the values of notes were found to be necessary, viz.: quarters, eighths, sixteenths, etc., when the longer values, ceasing to be employed, gradually disappeared."

New values were furthermore obtained by joining notes with a tie ⌒, and by placing a dot (.) after a note. Bars | | came into use, and with them compositions were divided into regular measures based upon the principles of modern-timed division (Germ. "Takt").

This latter innovation, resulting from the musical imitation and application of poetical *metre*, together with the introduction of rhythmical accentuation, were the most important and vital points in the emancipation of the old, and in the transformation of the old into our present music.

Music had at last become equal to all artistic requirements, and a scope of hitherto undreamed of magnitude was opened to the imagination of the composer.

It may not be out of place to show here in what manner modern music, through the imitation and adoption of poetical metre, attained in a great measure the logical and almost perfect metric-rhythmical development it has at present.

COMPARATIVE TABLE OF POETICAL METRE AND MUSICAL MEASURE.

Poetry	*Music*
is the rhythmical arrangement of articulated sounds (*i. e.*, syllables), into regulated succession of groups called METRES.	is the rhythmical arrangement of unarticulated sounds (*i. e.*, tones) into regulated succession of groups called MEASURES.

These depended,

in the classic languages, upon the way in which long and short syllables were made to succeed each other, *i. e.*, on QUANTITY.	in ancient music, upon the metres of poetry with which they were identical, *i. e.*, on QUANTITY; the long and short syllables being represented by long and short tones respectively.

They now depend,

In modern languages, (as in English,) upon the distinction of accented and unaccented syllables, *i. e.,*	In modern music, on both
On Quality.	*Quantity* and *Quality.*
	(See functions of rhythm.)

Thus, in the lines of :

1. Be′tter | fi′fty | yea′rs of | Eu′rope. |

Thus, in the measures :

1.  etc.

2. Bi′rd of the | wi′lderness, | bli′thesome and | cu′mberless. |

2.  etc.

The accents occur at regular intervals, and the groups

Of Syllables,   *Of Notes,*

thus formed, constitute each :

A *metre,* or foot.	A *measure.*
1st line, a trochee,	1st line, simple dual time.
2d line, a dactyle.	2d line, simple triple time.

Every modern metre contains an accented syllable, and one or two unaccented syllables.

As the accent may be on the first, second, or third syllable of a group, there thus arise five distinct measures, or feet :

and

two dissyllabic,

three trisyllabic,

as shown in the words :

Every modern measure contains one strong part which is accented, and one or two weak parts which are not accented.

As the accent always makes the beginning of a measure, there thus result two distinct measures, or times :

and

one dual,

one triple,

as shown in the groups :

(DISSYLLABIC),

1. fo′lly—corresponding to the classic trochee,

2. reca′ll—corresponding to the classic iambus.

SIMPLE DUAL TIME.

(From the fact that the accent always falls on the first part of the measure arises the necessity of beginning some movements with only part of a measure.)

(Trisyllabic).

3. ter′rible—dactyle,

4. confu′sion—amphibrachys,

5. absentee′—anapaest.

Four or more syllabic metres are mixtures and combinations of the above.

(*Chambers.*)

Simple Triple Time.

Two measures of simple dual time combined, make compound dual time:

Two, three, or four measures of simple triple time combined make compound triple time ; for example :

The rhythmical means of musical expression are naturally far richer than those of poetical expression.

Language has only one positive length and one positive shortness in its syllables, while in music any note may be length, because it may again be subdivided, and thus a shorter note obtained.

For example, an eighth (♪), being shorter than a quarter (♩) or a half (𝅗𝅥), is a long note compared to a sixteenth (𝅘𝅥𝅯) or a thirty-second (𝅘𝅥𝅰).

And any note may be shortness, because it may be doubled and thus obtain a longer note.

For example, a quarter (♩), being longer than an eighth (♪) or a sixteenth (𝅘𝅥𝅯), is a short note compared to a half (𝅗𝅥) or a whole note (𝅝).

This multiplicity of values makes it possible to represent musically every single foot of verse in almost infinite variety. See, for example, the trochee, a dissyllabic foot consisting of a long and a short syllable, — ‿.

Taking two short notes for one long syllable, the trochee can be musically represented in triple measure, viz.:

in $\frac{3}{2}$ | | etc.;

in $\frac{3}{4}$ | | etc.;

in $\frac{3}{8}$ | | etc.;

in $\frac{3}{16}$ | | etc.

Here are a few rhythmical varieties of the trochee, as represented by a $\frac{3}{4}$ measure:

$\frac{3}{4}$ etc.

When quality measuring is added, i. e., measuring by accented and unaccented parts, the facilities for varying the rhythmical means of representing musically the above trochee (or any other metre) are still greater.

An accented note stands for a long note, and thus the feet of verse can be imitated in a twofold way, viz.:

Dissyllabic metres, for example, — ‿, can be represented by simple dual time, $\frac{2}{4}$, and also by simple triple time, $\frac{3}{4}$. In both ways in endless variety.

And trisyllabic metres, for example, — ‿ ‿, can be represented by simple triple time, $\frac{3}{4}$, and also by both compound and simple dual time, $\frac{4}{4}$, or $\frac{2}{4}$, etc.

It would be, in fact, mathematically impossible to enumerate all the rhythmical varieties in which a single foot of verse could be musically represented.

The subject of rhythm is so intermixed by most theorists with the teachings of metric, that the greater number of musicians do not make a distinction between these two entirely different elements. This distinction was even less frequently made, before the appearance (in 1853) of Hauptmann's celebrated work, " Die Natur der Harmonik und der Metrik," and (in 1858) of Köhler's " Systematische Lehrmethode." But it is so plainly proved by these writers, that it would seem as logical to consider melody and harmony one element, as to consider rhythm and metric as one and the same thing.

METRIC. (Germ. *Metrik.*)

" An epithet applied by the ancient Greeks to that part of their prosody which had for its object the letters, syllables, feet, and verses of the poem.   The metric differed from the rhythmic in that the former was used only in the *form* of the verses, while the latter was confined to the *feet* of which they were composed."

Ancient music being governed by, and constructed according to, the laws of prosody, the term applied equally to music.

Metric may be defined as prescribing the laws of metre, and also of constructing musical periods.—(" *Die Lehre vom Versmass und vom musikalischen Periodenbau.*")

Rhythmic, as prescribing the laws of rhythm.

Metre is the precise measure according to which the rhythmic motion in language and in music is regulated.

Rhythm is the particular nature of the motion within this measure.

The following terms being often used indiscriminately, I will classify them to avoid confusion hereafter.

Metre, measure, metrum are synonymous, expressing the idea of precise measure in a generic sense.*

Foot, time, tact are synonymous, expressing the same idea specifically.

Metre and *foot* (English) are used in reference to poetry.

Measure and *time* (English) ⎱
Metrum and *tact* (German) ⎰ are used in reference to music.

---

* When speaking of musical measure in a generic sense, the German (or Latin) term "metrum" is more precise than the English "measure," because the latter is also used specifically, as, for example, " $\frac{2}{4}$ measure," " $\frac{3}{4}$ measure," etc.   When particularizing the metrum, the German word "tact" is also more precise and less ambiguous than the English "time," because the latter is used likewise in the sense of tempo.   I shall, therefore, use the German terms wherever the meaning might be doubtful.

Metrum is as indispensable to and dependent on rhythm, as rhythm is on metrum. Both must go together.

Metrum is the form, the vessel containing the rhythm.

Rhythm is the matter, the contents so measured by metrum.

Rhythm without metrum is motion without system.

Metrum without rhythm is system without motion.

To symbolize in simple form the difference between metrum and rhythm, let us consider the time-beating of a conductor, to indicate the metrum (specifically the tact), and the playing of the notes (melody and harmony not considered) to be the rhythm.   Thus,

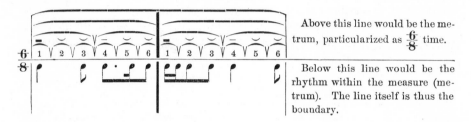

Above this line would be the metrum, particularized as $\frac{6}{8}$ time.

Below this line would be the rhythm within the measure (metrum). The line itself is thus the boundary.

Rhythm is the ever-changing, volatile motion which in its formation can be of endless variety.

Measure is the never-changing, steady form or principle which holds in check and directs the timed division of its motion.

Rhythm is the product of fantasy.

Measure requires no fantasy.

A measure of music is, by its nature, the unit of metric, as a whole note is the unit of rhythm.

Both these units are divisible into either *two* or *three* parts, with this difference, however :

The parts of the rhythmic unit are re-divisible into halves, quarters, eighths, etc., to the smallest practicable fractions.

The parts of the metrical unit are not again divisible ; but the unit is to be multiplied (by either two or three).

The division and subdivisions of the whole note, into halves, quarters, eighths, sixteenths, etc., give to the rhythmic motion the means of infinite variety.

The division of the measure into dual or triple parts, particularizes the measure.

Hence arises "*the tact.*"

The tact (time) specifies these dual or triple parts of the measure as so many quarters, eighths, or other rhythmic values. The dual or triple parts constituting a measure may be either simple or compound.   Thus arise four distinct kinds of measure, viz.:

Simple dual measure, specified in the tact as $\frac{2}{2}, \frac{2}{4}, \frac{2}{8}, \frac{2}{16}.$

Simple triple measure,   "   "   " $\frac{3}{2}, \frac{3}{4}, \frac{3}{8}, \frac{3}{16}.$

Compound dual measure,   "   "   " $\frac{4}{2}, \frac{4}{4}, \frac{4}{8}, \frac{4}{16},$ etc.

Compound triple measure, "   "   " $\frac{6}{8}, \frac{9}{8}, \frac{12}{8},$ etc.

Besides prescribing the measure of rhythm, metric has also the other function of prescribing the construction of periods.

In the former function the metrical unit (the measure) is divided into parts; in the latter function the metrical unit is *multiplied* and formed into symmetrical time-groups.

These symmetrical time-groups are formed by uniting

Two measures into a group called a section (two measures).
Two sections into another group called a phrase (four measures).
Two phrases into a larger group called a period (eight measures).

A period is, in music, what a sentence is in grammar; it contains a complete thought.

A number of periods form a part (movement, Satz, Act), and several parts constitute a whole work.

This system of forming measures into symmetrical time-groups, terminating in the period, and of building up a musical work with periods, has caused, and entitles, metric to be aptly styled "*the architectonic of music.*"

Art has as its fundamental law the law of beauty.

Beauty presupposes symmetry.

Symmetry is visible rhythm.

Rhythm is audible symmetry, or symmetrical motion.

Symmetrical motion is the ground-element of music.

Reciting from page 32.   "'It seems to be a necessity for man, if movements of any kind are to be sustained for a length of time,' that, instead of an undivided flow, the movement should be divided into parts, and 'that some more or less strict law of interchange should regulate the succession of these parts.'"

The first of these conditions is fulfilled by metric and **rhythm**, metric dividing a composition into symmetrical time-groups, periods, measures; and rhythm dividing the contents of the measures into parts, the parts into smaller parts, and so on *ad infinitum.*

The latter condition is fulfilled by the *accents* of metrum and rhythm. These accents form the needed law of interchange, which regulates the succession of the parts.

Both metrical and rhythmical accents—in order to fulfil their functions —must obey the grammatical principle of accentuation, which consists in bringing into prominence the first out of every two or three parts.

Metrical accents do this with measures; rhythmical accents, with parts of measures.

PART I.

RHYTHMICAL ACCENTS.

I DISTINGUISH two classes of rhythmical accents—

GRAMMATICAL ACCENTS;
CHARACTERISTIC ACCENTS.

The grammatical accents bring out the grammatical points of rhythm, *i. e.*, they make prominent one out of two, or one out of three parts, in every rhythmical division.

The characteristic accents bring out the characteristic points of rhythm, *i. e.*, they make prominent certain rhythmical peculiarities which portray something characteristic in the rhythm.

1. Grammatical Accents.

The first part in every rhythmical division demands, as Hauptmann calls it, " the energy of beginning;" hence, the first is the strong part, requiring to be distinguished from the second and third, or weak parts, by accent.

This principle is an integral portion of rhythm itself, and constitutes the grammatical principle of rhythmic accentuation.

Grammatical accents are either

a. POSITIVE, or *b.* NEGATIVE.

They are *positive*, when given on the strong part of any rhythmical division, and

They are *negative*, when given on a weak part of any rhythmical division.

The positive accents are normal, establishing the rule; the negative accents are abnormal, departing from the rule.

CHAPTER I.

POSITIVE GRAMMATICAL ACCENTS.

ACCORDING to the generally accepted opinion, the object of these accents is to denote the measure.

The real object, however, according to the present theory, is to denote the strong part in every rhythmical division, *i. e.*, the first out of every *two* or *three* parts.

The marking of the time is thus not the direct object of grammatical accents, but the indirect one; the natural consequence of grammatical principles.

This distinction will hereafter be the subject of special discussion.

Rhythmical division divides a note into two or three smaller notes. But, inasmuch as a triplet counts only as much as two notes of their kind, rhythmical division produces virtually a pair only.

The relative importance of such pairs depends on the division to which they belong.

The pair produced by first division is more important than the pairs belonging to the second division. Those of the second division are more important than those belonging to the third, and so on.

Louis Köhler explains the relative importance of rhythmical pairs, hence the relative force of their accents, by comparing rhythmic division to a family.

The first division, or pair, he likens to male and female, to symbolize the strong and weak. And so on, in every new division, each pair is male and female.

He does not, however, enlighten us as to the gender of the unit of rhythm—the whole note, from which all division emanates.

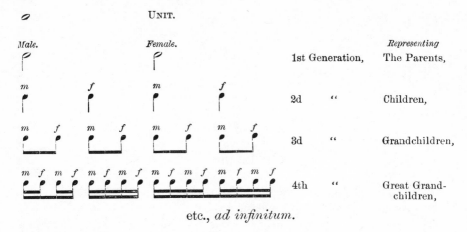

etc., *ad infinitum.*

In triple division (following Köhler's idea) the first part of the triplet is the male; the second and third, females, which renders the family relation a little mixed.

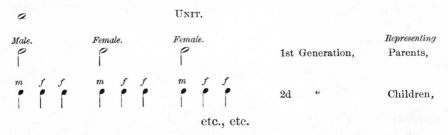

etc., etc.

It is evident that, with every new division, or generation, the accents of the pairs (or triplets) become less significant, less strong; and yet the principle of distinguishing the strong from the weak is always the same.

This distinction is as essential in music as syllabic accentuation is in language.

Syllabic accentuation, when wrongly given, omitted, or exaggerated, is at once remarked; but, when rightly given, is simply felt, and not noticed.

It is the same with grammatical accents.

They would be missed when omitted, objectionable when wrongly given or exaggerated; and should be present, but not predominant, simply felt without being remarked. They should pervade a musical composition, as the beating of the pulse pervades whatsoever has life, because they give a swinging, undulating, human element to a movement, which would be stiff and machine-like, lacking in pulsation and life, without them.

This is why a music-box and a barrel-organ, though mechanically correct, are so tiresome and monotonous.

It is, of course, not necessary to observe every one of these accents, especially not those of the smaller divisions.

Although the rule implies that the first out of every two or three parts, however small the parts may be, is to be accented, it would be utterly opposed to every idea of beauty, if this rule were observed with absolute strictness.

The very principle which demands this grammatical rule suggests its modification.

Taking this rule to the letter would restrict all rhythmic motion to a stiffness and dryness almost as detrimental to beauty as the monotony of not at all accenting, which it is the object of grammatical accents to avert.

But taking this rule according to its spirit prevents this stiffness, and gives the rule a far wider scope than it had before.

In every pair, of whatever value, whether , , , or , the first, as the strong part, is accented.

But, when two pairs are joined, the pair produced by this joining is of greater significance than the members of each separate pair. Hence, the great pair is accented, and the accents on the smaller pairs recede; for example:

And again, if twice two pairs are joined, the double pairs forming a group are of greater moment than the single pairs. Hence, the groups are accented, and the accents on the pairs recede; for example:

The same, with groups of more than four notes; for example:

Here already the minor accents disappear, and yet the spirit of grammatical rule is observed.

4

In the case of triplets, quintuplets, sextuplets, septuplets, or other groups of whatever number of notes, the grammatical principle is substantially the same as in pairs, although there is some slight difference in appearance; for example:

A Triplet has these accents,

The first note, forming a pair with the second, has "the energy of beginning,"

The second note, forming a pair with the third, has prominence over the third,

The third note is altogether the weak and unaccented part of the triplet.

And further: The first pair has prominence over the second pair,

Therefore, the first note has a double accent, the second note has a single accent, and the third note has no accent at all,

In a Sextuplet, the accents depend on whether the sextuplet arises from a pair or from a triplet.

A true sextuplet arises from a triplet, and is accented as a triplet; for example:

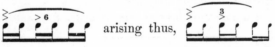 arising thus,

A false sextuplet arises from a pair, and is accented as a pair; for example:

 arising thus, or

A Quintuplet, being the combination of a pair and a triplet, or a triplet and a pair, is accented accordingly,

 either so, or so,

A SEPTUPLET, being the combination of a triplet and a quadruplet, or a quadruplet and triplet, is accented

either so,   or so,

A NONUPLET, being the triple compound of a triplet, is accented like a single triplet,

either so,   or so,

A group of twelve notes, being the compound of either dual or triple roots, is accented, according to the roots, in four ways :

TRIPLET ROOTS. { 1. As a Pair,

2. As a Quadruplet,

DUAL ROOTS. { 3. As a Triplet,

4. As a Sextuplet,

Groups of ten, eleven, thirteen, fourteen, or a greater number of notes, are accented on the same principle, according to the dual or triple roots which the rhythm suggests.

In complicated cases, where these roots do not suggest themselves readily, the performer should analyze the numbers, in order to arrive at the roots. When these have been found, the groups are subdivided accordingly, and the accents, when agreeing with the subdivision, will then be correctly given.

It is, of course, neither necessary to dissect every group or passage to its primary root, nor is it expedient to accent every pair or triplet. Too much subdivision, although rendering the rhythm very distinct, would be detrimental to fluency, as too much accentuation would impede velocity.

A few suggestions may serve as general directions. The slower the tempo, the more minutely may these accents be observed ; (see, for exam-

ple, Beethoven's Sonata Pathetique, where this ♪, in the Grave movement, is equal to the ◔, in the Allegro,) while in a quick tempo the
chief accents only should be marked, and these even with due digression.

The division of passages depends not alone on grammatical, but also
on melodic and harmonic as well as metrical considerations, and also on
time and tempo.

Attention must here be called to one particular point. When dividing
into parts, groups of notes containing a combination of dual and triple
roots: for example, a quintulet or septulet, one of the parts must
necessarily have a greater number of notes than the other.

Now the question arises: Shall the larger number come first, or last?
To decide this, depends on the following conditions:

1. *Rhythmically.* When the motion is increasing, the larger number comes last; when
   decreasing, the larger number comes first.
2. *Melodic.* The rhythmic division should be in accordance with the melodic formation, in
   such manner, that not only the notes are played in time and tempo, but a melodic
   idea be brought out in plastic prominence.
3. *Harmonic.* To avoid wrong progressions with the counterparts, the division should
   also take into consideration the accompaniment and the counterparts.

With all due respect to the great pianoforte composers, from Mozart to
Chopin, it is quite plain, that, in point of rhythmic notation, the old
masters were often very inexact and careless; and we have to be very
thankful, that the old laxity of rhythmic notation, notably of grouping together a long row of notes without any distinct division, is more and more
disappearing.

Rhythmic interpretation, of Chopin's passages, for example, is often a
sore puzzle, and rarely quite clear to the average player. And how could
this be otherwise, seing that frequently a whole passage is suspended, so to
say, on the hook of a single note:

Mozart, Hummel, and their contemporaries, even Beethoven, the
great master of rhythm, the minutely exact, conformed to the custom of
their time, and wrote numbers of undivided passages and cadenzas,
leaving them to be interpreted *ad libitum.* Unfortunately, the latitude

thus given is not calculated either to facilitate or to improve the reading. On the contrary, the result is more often that of puzzling the performer, than of aiding the performance.

Modern composers (whatever the contents of their compositions may be) endeavor at least to make their rhythmic notation plain and accurate. Many of the old abbreviations—for instance, the numerous signs for ornamentation—are now generally written in full; and passages, cadenzas, arabesques, are no longer left to the individual fancy of the interpreter, but are represented clearly and unmistakably.

Thanks to the many careful and masterly revisions of the classics, notably Von Bülow's, and to some of the new Chopin editions, the old *ad libitum* style of interpretation (in rhythmic respect), which only too often resembled the unsteady gait of a drunken man, is giving way to positiveness and precision, as far as rhythm is concerned. And that pernicious *rubato* nuisance, that slippery downward course in time-keeping, which Chopin's disciples and unripe admirers are greatly responsible for, is happily becoming rarer and scarcer.

A few examples of the old looseness in rhythmic notation, as compared with modern accuracy, will explain the great advantage of the latter and the need of representing precisely and unmistakably the composer's ideas in their correct rhythmic garb. The following illustrations from Chopin, Hummel, and Beethoven will explain this more particularly:

CHOPIN—Polonaise, Op. 26, No. 1.

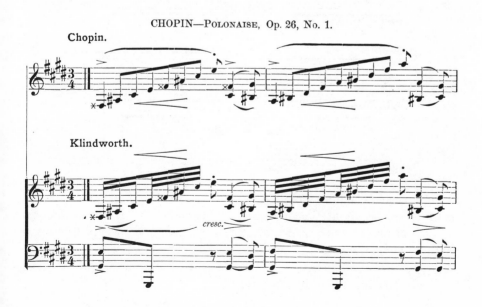

Simple and natural as these passages appear when divided, every teacher knows that, in their original notation, they are by no means clear to the average player.

CHOPIN—VALSE, Op. 34, No. 1.

CHOPIN—POLONAISE, Op. 71.

Comparing Chopin's notation with Klindworth's, the latter, because more precise, is unquestionably easier to comprehend. If the advantage of such precise notation over the author's less precise one is apparent even in these simple examples, the advantage is certainly much more palpable in the great number of more complicated cases, which the original editions leave in undisturbed uncertainty.

CHOPIN—Nocturne, Op. 32, No. 1.

Let rigorous musicians grumble at such innovations, on the ground that those who attempt to play Chopin should be sufficiently advanced to interpret his rhythm, each one according to his own conception, thus leaving room for many different ways, and not keeping to one particular idea or precept.

It may, however, be replied, that a player who is so far advanced in maturity and intelligence, as to be able independently and correctly to interpret Chopin, is himself the best judge whether or not he will accept Klindworth's, or any other editor's, rhythmical interpretation; while those who are not so far advanced—and their number is by far the greater —will unquestionably derive a great benefit by having pointed out to them positively what would otherwise have been doubtful.

We cannot blame Chopin for writing his passages and cadenzas in a loose, indefinite manner, inasmuch as he followed the custom of his time, according to which his notation was quite natural and correct. Hummel, his predecessor, was much more inexact.

The following examples from Hummel's A-minor Concerto are extracts from H. Germer's "Rhythmische Probleme."

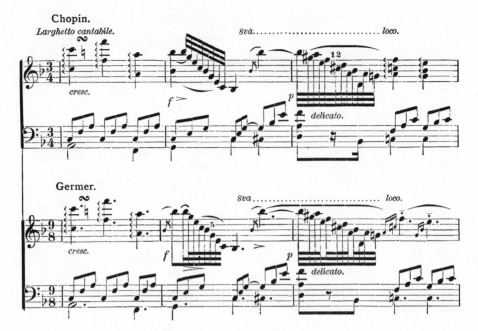

Chopin.
Larghetto cantabile.

Germer.

The changed time ($\frac{9}{8}$) is far more in keeping with the rhythm of this movement than the composer's indicated $\frac{3}{4}$ time, and renders a precise rhythmic division not only possible, but quite easy; compare, for example, the accompaniments of the third measure.

HUMMEL—Concerto in A-Minor.

Original.
Larghetto Cantabile.

Amended by Germer.

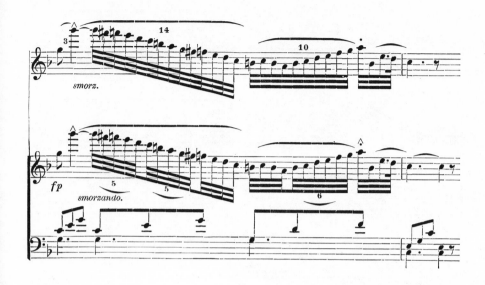

Original.

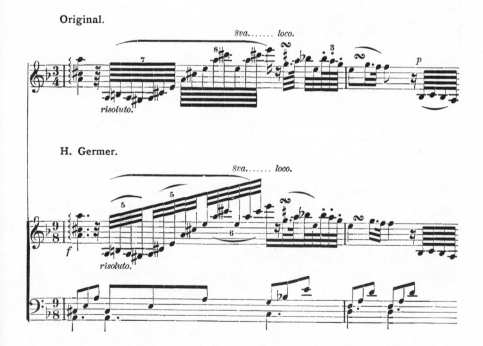

H. Germer.

Comparing the original notation with the revised version, the superiority of the latter in explicitness, and hence in clearness, is so evident as to need no comment.

Beethoven, the pattern of exactness in almost every particular, is generally most accurate in mechanical details, and yet we find in his pianoforte compositions, as in those of his contemporaries, a great number of passages and cadenzas written in a long row of undivided notes, to be interpreted *ad libitum*.

Far from criticising this historical custom, and recognizing even a certain utility—though to the *master*-performer only—in the latitude thus given, I would call the attention of the reader to the following examples which show the manner of Beethoven's notation as compared with Dr. Von Bülow's revision. The reader may then draw his own conclusion as to which of these two notations is the more comprehensible and useful, and hence the more desirable.

BEETHOVEN—SONATA, Op. 27, No. 2.

BEETHOVEN—SONATA, Op. 27, No. 1.

SONATA, Op. 27, No. 1.

See also the cadenza of Beethoven's Sonata, Op. 31, in G-major, as exemplified in the chapter of Dynamics, page 245.

BEETHOVEN—Concerto, Op. 58, in G-major.

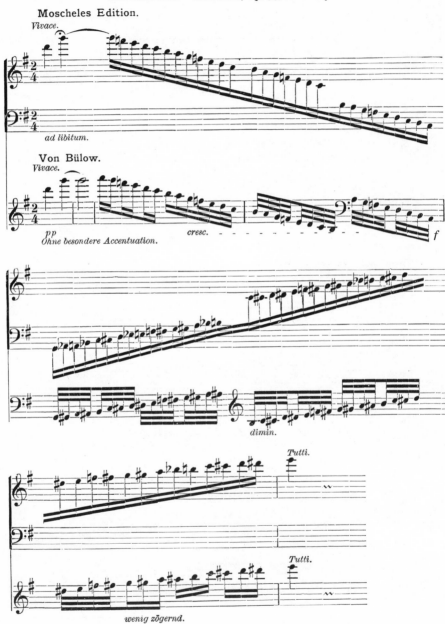

The only advantage which is to be recognized in *free* rhythmical interpretation over positive reading, based upon precise rhythmical division, is that the former (at the hands of a master) may be accomplished in many different ways; while the latter is limited to the indicated way alone.

But this is no argument against precise notation.

As it is the performer's duty to render faithfully the composer's work according to the latter's indications, so it should be the composer's duty to clothe his ideas in such accurate rhythmic garb as to leave no doubt of their meaning. When this is done, no musician would add to, or retouch, those ideas. But let there be a question of doubt, and every one, whether qualified or not, will interpret the composer's meaning according to his own notion or fancy, generally more to detriment than to advantage of the composition.

This should not be. Hence, it is better to have all doubtful cases interpreted by a master rather than to leave them to the mercy of every petty musician or amateur.

These remarks and illustrations, although apparently digressing from the main subject, have a direct bearing upon it, because the accented and unaccented parts of any rhythmic motion cannot be ascertained with any certainty, unless the rhythm is judiciously divided.

I now return to positive grammatical accents, more particularly to *their relation to the time.*

We know that positive grammatical accents have the object of giving prominence to the first out of two or three parts in every division, and that the relative importance of these accents depends on the division to which they belong.

To be more definite, I designate as

> *Primary*—the accent of the 1st rhythmical division ; as
> *Secondary*—the accents of the 2d division ; as
> *Tertiary*—those of the 3d division, and so on.

The exact dynamic force of these different grades cannot be stated, and I can only attempt to convey an approximate idea of the relative quality of these accents.

The quality of primary accents bears about the same proportion to that of secondary ones as three bears to two; or one might say, the former have not quite twice the dynamic force of the latter.

This proportion remains in subsequent accents.

Now, to connect the object of grammatical accents with their time-denoting effect, it is sufficient to point out the fact that their object is identical with that of the so-called " measure-accents," viz., to denote the strong time-parts.

It would thus appear, that one or the other kind of these accents is superfluous.

Let us see, which.

Measure-accents, although denoting the specified time-parts, do not go beyond them.

Grammatical accents, however, denote these time-parts equally well, and, moreover, penetrate to the smallest rhythmical details.

The latter, therefore, go far beyond the reach of the former and must, at all events, be retained, while the former can well be omitted.

But, in rejecting measure-accents (as a separate class) and accepting only grammatical ones, a theoretical impediment (although but a hair-splitting one) presents itself.

According to a previous statement,

The measure is metrical, the contents of the measure rhythmical.

The former is unanimously accepted; the latter statement has met with the objection that the specified measure-parts are metrical, and only the parts of these parts rhythmical.

Hauptmann, " Natur der Harmonik und Metrik," also *Köhler*, " Systematische Lehrmethode," express their opinion substantially as follows :

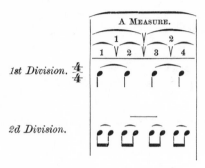

1st Division. $\frac{4}{4}$

This measure contains four metrical parts, specified as quarters, forming two pairs, each pair having an accent on its strong part.

(These accents would be the measure-accents, and as such metrical.)

2d Division.

Here begins the first rhythmical division forming four pairs, each having a *rhythmical* accent on its strong part.

According to this conception (against the logic of which nothing can be said), rhythmical division, hence rhythmical accents, would commence with the second division of the measure, instead of with the first. In other words: rhythmic division would start from the measure-*parts*, instead of having the full value of the measure as unit.

Without disputing the theoretical correctness of such a discrimination, it may be confidently asserted, that there are as many and as good reasons for holding the contents of the measure to be entirely rhythmical, as for considering them to be merely partially so. The plea of metrical time-parts is but a hair-splitting, theoretical distinction, without any real difference; it is certainly without the least practical importance, and is actually the great hindrance to a complete rhythmical accent-system.

The present theory, though admitting the measure-parts to be metrical, in the sense of a passive principle (*i. e.*, theoretically), yet holds them to be rhythmical in the sense of active life, (*i. e.*, practically).

Hence, in order to do away with unnecessary complication, it does not acknowledge metrical measure-accents at all, and knows only rhythmic-grammatical accents within the measure.

Embodying the above opinions in one fundamental principle, I pronounce *the contents of the measure to be wholly and purely rhythmical;* consequently, the measure-parts are also rhythmical, and their accents likewise. In this view, I consider the full prescribed measure-value to be the unit for rhythmical division, and I divide the measure, immaterial whether simple or compound, as rhythm divides any given value, viz. :

First division, into one pair   (or triplet) ;
Second division, into two pairs (or triplets) ;
Third division, into four pairs (or triplets); and so on.

Every measure, whether simple or compound, has accordingly only :

One primary strong part—One primary grammatical accent ;
Two secondary strong parts—Two secondary grammatical accents ;
Four tertiary strong parts—Four tertiary grammatical accents ; and so on.

The following examples will explain these divisions and their corresponding accents more minutely :

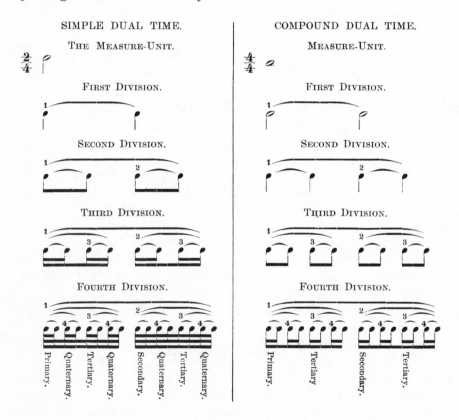

It is self-evident, that, when two or more accents of different grade fall together on the same note, the more important accent takes precedence, and causes the less important ones to recede.

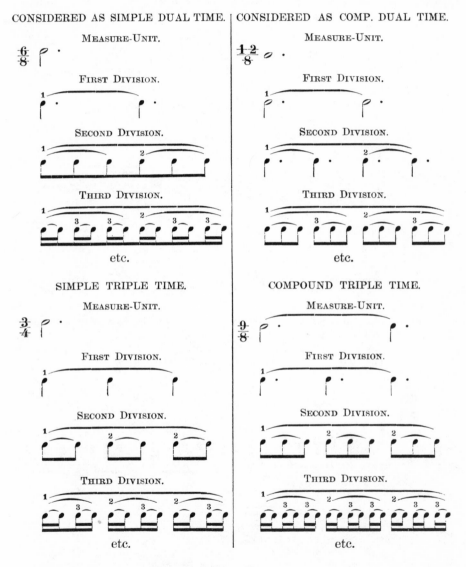

CONSIDERED AS SIMPLE DUAL TIME.   CONSIDERED AS COMP. DUAL TIME.

SIMPLE TRIPLE TIME.   COMPOUND TRIPLE TIME.

The chief point in the present system of grammatical accents, the point which alone made such a system possible, is to consider the full pre-scribed measure-value as the rhythmical unit. Apart from the fact, that

5

the usual measure-accents thus become superfluous, the present system also removes the unnecessary distinction (made by Hauptmann and Köhler) between quadruple time and double dual division; and likewise does away with the accentual distinction of simple and compound time.

Applied to pianoforte playing, this system is as simple as it is indispensable. It enables the performer to regulate with facility and precision the different grades of grammatical accents, from the chief measure-parts down to the smallest rhythmical details, in full consciousness of their relative importance.

A few illustrations will sufficiently demonstrate this.

CHOPIN—Etude, Op. 10, No. 3.

The numbers designate the relative importance of the parts and their accents.

MENDELSSOHN—Rondo capriccioso, Op. 14,

BEETHOVEN—SONATA, Op. 26.

Observe the dynamic difference of the two cases, otherwise similar, indicated by the asterisks ✻.

It is not necessary to further extend those illustrations, inasmuch as any piece of music taken at random answers the purpose equally well.

Only let it be remembered, that grammatical accentuation is as necessary in accompaniment as in melody; for example:

The technical difficulty of dynamical discrimination in touch is probably the only difficulty in grammatical accentuation. This, however, like all technical matter, it is not in our province to discusss. Yet it may be remarked, that discrimination of touch must necessarily be preceded by perception, because, without the directing consciousness of the required degree of force, no precise degree of force can be attained by touch alone.

This needed consciousness in touch has been already, in some measure, supplied through the grading of accents, and will receive still further definition through more detailed explanations in the subsequent chapter on " Dynamics."

One thing remains to be said, a repeated warning against overdoing both in reference to the number of accents and the exaggeration of their dynamic degree.

Moderate and gentle accentuation is always more artistic and effective than strong and violent emphasis; and it would certainly be a less conspicuous fault, to omit an accent altogether, than to exaggerate it.

Primary accents should not be omitted, nor secondary ones in slow movements, though they may be omitted in quick tempo or where velocity is required. Tertiary and subsequent accents are of less importance.

I need not further comment upon the general necessity of grammatical accents, both as musical pulses and time-indicators; but I may add that discrimination of touch, which these accents require, is in itself one of the most beautiful attributes of pianoforte playing, and the dynamical finger-exercises, which are needed for the attainment of such discrimination, one of the best studies and an excellent method for refining and beautifying touch.

Discrimination of touch is the intellectual, the internal part of technique; finger velocity, only the mechanical, the external portion. Unfortunately, the majority of people are more influenced by external appearances than by internal worth. And so it is, that we have a crowd of pianoforte-players for whom technique is the chief ambition; and a large number of amateurs, who consider it more desirable to play runs and passages very fast and loudly, than to play them clearly and in moderate tempo, according to the player's capacity; who imagine that to play a long and difficult composition imperfectly, will advance them more in the estimation of their neighbors, than to play a small piece in a finished manner. Such people, although capable of running helter-skelter over a great deal of difficult ground, will have to a certainty a defective touch; it will be mechanically rough and uneven, and intellectually non-discriminating.

When, under judicious training, the rough edges of the touch are somewhat smoothed, and the intellectual part of touch, discrimination, is about to be taken up, it is then, that the teacher should insist on making the student observe positive grammatical accentuation *in all its dynamic details.*

The result of making him observe the requisite dynamic grading of rhythmical accents, is, as a rule, surprising, especially in reference to touch. And yet, *it is not so much the touch that will have changed and improved, as that the intelligence directing the touch will have been developed.*

The awakened consciousness of discrimination; the proper observance of accented and unaccented parts; the careful attention to grammatical principles—this A-B-C of musical expression—*these*, more than mechanical exercises, will have wrought the change.

CHAPTER II.

NEGATIVE GRAMMATICAL ACCENTS.

THESE accents, falling on the weak parts of a measure, are given negatively to grammatical rule, for the purpose of bringing variety into the rhythmic motion.

They have the same effect in rhythm that dissonances have in harmony; in fact, they constitute *the dissonances of rhythm*, as positive grammatical accents constitute the consonances of rhythm.

Æsthetically, this kind of accentuation is quite logical. Uninterrupted harmony would soon become as fatiguing as constant sunshine. A cloud, a storm, a dissonance—in fact, any kind of diversion—is generally a welcome change, a relief. Harmony, after discord, is a new pleasure; sunshine, after rain, gives fresh enjoyment. And so with rhythm.

A break in the rhythmic form gives more real animation to a movement and stronger evidence of artistic spirit, than strict observance of uniformity, or of positive rules, could possibly do.

Contrast, not uniformity, is a condition in every work of art. The petty artist, the mere scholar, will keep within the boundary of traditional rules; the great artist, the creator, the genius will go beyond them.

Haydn, dear, simple Haydn, was accused of employing too many dissonances. Beethoven, on this account, was called crazy, and the same fault was found with Schubert, Chopin, and Berlioz, and is now with Wagner.

As many and as great innovations have been made rhythmically as have taken place harmonically since the time of Haydn. Foremost among those who treated rhythm with the widest individuality and disregard of conventionalism were Chopin and Schumann, who both showed great partiality for rhythmical dissonances, especially Schumann.

Negative accents, although falling in direct opposition to grammatical rule, are still grammatical, because, paradoxical though it may seem, they are really positive accents, which by the composer's fancy have been *removed* from a strong to a weak part of the time.

The principle of considering negative grammatical accents as removed positive ones will greatly facilitate the conception and interpretation of many a complicated rhythm, and throw a light of peculiar interest upon many a mystifying notation.

I class negative accents into

> 1. Syncopic, and
> 2. Removed ones;

both being negative, both being removed positive accents.

i. Syncopic Accents.

Syncope (literally, a cutting off, or diminution) means, in music, a contraction.

It is a rhythmical device dating from classic Greek poetry, by which the long and short syllables of a metre, or the *arsis* and *thesis*, were contracted into one long syllable called " Syncope;" *i. e.*, the syncope fell on the *arsis* (or long syllable) and contained the *thesis* (or short syllable.)

During the period of the Gregorian chant, this arrangement was reversed, the syncope being there formed by the contraction of a weak and strong part, instead, as originally, of a strong and weak one.

The contrapuntists of the next period employed the syncope also harmonically and could do this logically, because what is rhythmically the strong or accented part corresponds harmonically to consonance, and what is rhythmically the weak or unaccented part corresponds harmonically to dissonance.

(The corresponding qualities are judged by the ear. The ear can rest satisfied rhythmically on a strong part, or harmonically on a consonance; it cannot rest satisfied rhythmically on a weak part, or harmonically on a dissonance.)

The syncope falling, in the Gregorian chant, on the weak or unaccented part of the measure, it would have been consistent in the contrapuntists to have made it fall on a corresponding dissonance. This, however, viz., the idea of carrying over the dissonance from a weak to a strong part, was repugnant to their feelings; therefore they resorted to the remedy of letting the syncope commence on a consonance and then become a dissonance. They called this " preparing " the dissonance; for example:

In modern music, syncopes are not restricted by any such considerations, but are altogether freely used.

They are always rhythmical and form one value only, through the contraction of an unaccented and accented note or notes.

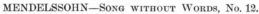

They may appear on either consonance or dissonance; for example:

MENDELSSOHN—Song without Words, No. 12.

In *anticipation* of the chord to which the syncope belongs; for example:

BEETHOVEN—Sonata, Op. 27, No. 2.

or in *retardation* of the chord to which they belong.

SCHUMANN—Davidsbündler, No. 4.

Syncopic accent, i. e., the special stress which is laid on the syncope, is given for the following reasons:

Every syncope consists of two notes contracted into one.

The regular accent which is due on the second of these notes is impossible, because this second note is tied ⌢ to the first.

The accent is, therefore, thrown forward and given in *anticipation,* for example, ♪ | ♪ . Such anticipation removes the accent from a strong to a weak part, causing the syncope to fall negatively to grammatical rule. The syncope thus produces a dissonance in the rhythmic flow of the movement, but brings through that dissonance variety into the rhythm.

NOTE.—Another explanation is this : The syncope being a contraction of two notes, making one long note, is accented by reason of its *quantity*—

$$\frac{4}{4} \ \hat{\rho} \ \overset{\wedge}{\overset{\frown}{\rho}} \ \rho \ | = \rho \ \overset{\wedge}{\rho} \ \rho \ |$$

while the regular accent is given on *quality*. (See Functions of Rhythm, page 33. Also, Quantitative Accents, page 171.)

The rhythm is often, by means of syncopation, completely changed, as in cases like this: $\frac{3}{4}$ ♪ ♪ : ♪ | ♪ : ♪ ♪ | . The effect being $\frac{2}{4}$ within $\frac{3}{4}$, or dual within triple time: $\frac{2}{4}$ ♪ ♪ | ♪ | ♪ ♪ |

For example, in the following illustration from Beethoven's Eroica Symphony,

the effect is dual rhythm within triple time.

This example serves likewise to illustrate what the Italians call an "*imbroglio*," or confusion, meaning rhythmical confusion.

An imbroglio is caused by irregular accentuation, sometimes by syncopation, but more frequently by the intermingling of several voices, each voice accenting its phrases independently, as though a room full of people were talking together at the same time, the result being that the grammatical accents are no longer to be detected by the ear.   Hence, a rhythmical confusion.

Syncopation is also effectively employed in accompaniments, while the melody is not syncopic; for example:

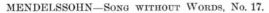

MENDELSSOHN—Song without Words, No. 17.

Or in the melody, while the accompaniment is regular.

SCHUMANN—Carnival.

Very striking and effective examples of this manner of syncopation are to be found in the valses of Strauss, Lanner, etc.

The last example again illustrates how syncopation can completely change the rhythm.   It also shows (by the dotted lines, ⋮ ⋮) in   what manner negative (syncopic) accents may be replaced—moved back, so to say—and become positive accents.

Similar replacements of removed accents occur sometimes by themselves; for example:

SCHUBERT—MOMENS MUSICAUX, Op. 94, No. 4.

This movement continues for fifty-two measures with the same rhythmical regularity.   The " *Schwerpunkt*," or centre of gravity, so to say, in each measure, which is here the syncope, cannot fail before long to assert itself, causing the accents to fall naturally upon the ear, as though the measure were divided as is indicated by the dotted lines.

I will here cite a paragraph from Hauptmann's " Natur der Harmonik und Metrik," which has an especial bearing upon this and similar cases:

If a row (of notes) is to appear syncopic, another non-syncopic one should exist; because without the normal row, to which the syncopic one forms the contrast, the latter would appear as being itself normally accented, and this line:

would appear thus :

This will explain how the replacement of certain syncopic accents occurs sometimes by itself.

2. Removed Accents.

This term (or " verschobene," as the Germans call them,) is really another name only for negative accents; all negative accents being removed positive ones, and all removed accents being negative.   I shall, nevertheless, employ the above term in a specific, instead of a general sense, for those negative accents which are *non*-syncopic.

Let us see in what way removed accents differ from the syncopic ones.

Both affect the time negatively.

But, while syncopic accents bring out single negative points (syncopes) dissonating with the time individually, removed accents bring out combined negative points (phrases) dissonating with the time collectively.

Syncopes, being indicated by a tie, ⌒ = 𝄞, which contracts two notes into one negative point, dissonate with the time individually.

Rhythmical phrases, being indicated by a slur = 𝄞 etc., which contracts two or more notes into so many combined negative points, dissonate with the time collectively.

Further explanation is here indispensable, regarding

PHRASES.

Musical phrases resemble short sentences in language, and, like the latter, require to be distinguished by interpunction, in notation, and by accentuation and breath-taking, in delivery.

We recognize three kinds of phrases:

METRICAL, MELODIC, AND RHYTHMICAL.

It has already been mentioned, that a period of eight measures resembles a complete sentence, such as would be followed by a full stop (.).

A *metrical* phrase, consisting of at least four measures, is generally half a period, half a sentence, and would be followed by a semi-colon (;).

A *melodic* phrase is a short melodic sentence, or figure, formed by an unbroken succession of melodically arranged notes.

The extent or length of melodic phrases is not so much limited in number of notes, as in duration of time. Long phrases would be as awkward in music as in language; hence, even in instrumental music, melodic phrases do not exceed in length the duration of one breath.

Regarding interpunction, they resemble that part of a sentence which would be followed by a comma (,).

More about these phrases will be found under *Melodic Accents.*

A *rhythmical* phrase is a short rhythmical figure of two, three, four, or more notes, which is indicated by a slur, ⌒ (the only collective sign we possess); for example, 𝄞 or 𝄞 , etc.*

Several rhythmical phrases, when repeated (generally on different intervals), form together a melodic phrase; for example:

---

* A syncope, containing two notes contracted into *one* value, 𝄞 , is, of course, not a phrase, the latter requiring at least two different notes.

This example, as a whole, is a metrical phrase of four measures; it is also a melodic phrase, when the sound or pitch of the notes is taken into consideration.

BEETHOVEN—Sonata, Op. 14, No. 2.

Scherzo.

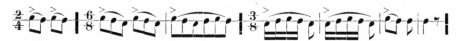

The first rhythmical figure, , which is three times repeated, is a rhythmical phrase; more particularly, a negative rhythmical phrase.

With the latter kind of phrases we have here especially to do.

Rhythmical phrases are either positive or negative. (The French use the terms "masculine" and "feminine.")

They are *positive*, when the first note falls on a strong part of the measure, and the rhythm agrees with the time; for example:

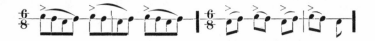

They are *negative*—

1. When the first note falls on a weak part of the measure, although the rhythm may be agreeing with the time; for example:

2. When the rhythm does not agree with the time, although the initial note may be falling on a strong time-part; for example:

The positive or negative character of rhythmical accents corresponds with the character of rhythmical phrases, in such a way, that positive phrases have positive accents, and negative (or removed) phrases have negative (or removed) accents.

Instead of further explanation, I subjoin a few illustrations of both kinds of negative (or removed) phrases, including their corresponding accents.

1. Negative or Removed Phrases, not opposed to the Time.

WEBER—SONATA IN D-MINOR.

WEBER—SONATA IN D-MINOR.

CHOPIN—ETUDE, Op. 10, No. 10.

BEETHOVEN—SONATA, Op. 10, No. 3 (in D-Major).

2. Negative or Removed Phrases, opposed to the Time.

WEBER—SONATA IN D-MINOR.

WEBER—SONATA IN D-MINOR.

BEETHOVEN—SONATA, Op. 31, No. 2 (in D-Minor).

These phrases are opposed to the time, because they denote a dual rhythm within triple measure.

WEBER—CONCERTSTÜCK.

And here, the phrases denote a triple rhythm within dual time.

Hoping that the respective terms, "negative," "syncopic," "removed accents," and "negative removed phrases," will have become quite clear to the student, I shall now, as a resumé of the foregoing, review the entire subject of negative accents by means of illustrations.

These examples will be arranged into three divisions, illustrating the three phases of negative accents.

FIRST PHASE OF NEGATIVE ACCENTS.

The rhythm being removed, but still agreeing with the time.

SCHUMANN—KREISLERIANA, No. 2.

In this example the rhythm is removed by anticipation. The strong part of the time is pushed forward, so to say, instead of falling naturally upon the beginning of the measure.

This is one of the phases of negative accents in which the negativeness appears more in notation than in effect; in which the removal is an uncalled for, useless whim of the composer, mystifying the reader, without being able to deceive the listener.

There is no reason for beginning this movement with an incomplete measure, since its character, its phrasing, and Schumann's own *forte*-marks plainly indicate that it ought to begin with the full measure.

If the student will disregard the indicated bars and substitute for them the dotted lines, ⋮ ⋮ , the accents will fall quite naturally upon the ear ; and the rhythm, being replaced in its natural position, will be more comprehensible, more clear.

Whereas, by strictly adhering to the bars, in blind veneration for the composer, the accentuation is abnormal and stiff, bizarre instead of natural, difficult to the performer, and little comprehensible to the listener.

SCHUMANN—Carnival.

An example similar to the former.

SCHUMANN—Fantasia, Op. 17 (C-major).

The accents are here removed through syncopation; but there was not the slightest occasion for syncopation. The abnormalism of such unnatural accentuation, which in this case is again an uncalled for, bizarre

mystification, could easily have been avoided, without the least detriment
to the composer's ideas or to the intended effect, by a plain notation like
the following :

SCHUMANN—Fantasia.

But it is almost a rule with Schumann to prefer a complicated to a
plain rhythmical notation. He frequently avoids the latter and invents
the former, simply to gratify a fancy for making the phrasing negative ;
or, perhaps, with the idea of rendering his thoughts more interesting by
obscure notation.

SCHUMANN—Faschingsschwank, Op. 26.

The first part of this movement has the above eight phrases, each one
of one measure.

The second part has these eight phrases, four times, or thirty-two
measures of similar texture.

Notwithstanding the positiveness of the rhythm, Schumann has persistently written all the phrases negatively by syncopation.

Of what use, let me ask, are here the syncopes?

Why has the rhythm been removed? Does the removal bring variety into the rhythm?

None whatever.

Does it enhance the effect, or render the idea more interesting?

Not at all.

The syncopes merely serve to make the reading awkward and obscure, while to the listener they fall quite naturally upon the ear.

To make these eight measures quite clear, without in the least detracting from, or altering the composer's idea, read them in the following way:

Altered Notation.

The second part, consisting of thirty-two measures, or four periods of eight measures each, should be simplified in the same way, with the additional alteration of changing the last two measures, in each of the four periods, into three measures of $\frac{2}{4}$ time, because the rhythm in those measures is dual, not triple; for example:

Altered Notation.

Second Period.

I simply advocate these suggested changes as an imaginary operation, which will be justified by its result, inasmuch as they cannot fail to facilitate the perception of the composer's idea, both to the performer and listener.

Further examples of this first phase are hardly necessary.

SECOND PHASE OF NEGATIVE ACCENTS.

The rhythm removed, and not in accordance with the time.

SCHUMANN—Abendmusik, Op. 99, No. 12,

The phrases clearly indicate the rhythm to be in dual time, and therefore opposed to the prescribed triple time.

The suggested change of bars, ⋮ ⋮ , brings both the rhythm and its accents in accordance with the time, or the time in accordance with the rhythm, which is the same thing.

SCHUMANN—Kreisleriana.

This is similar to the last example. A musician would at once comprehend the duality of the time, and accent accordingly; but the ordinary student, adhering to the prescribed triple time, is sure to find this accenting against the time a stumbling-block difficult to overcome.

SCHUMANN—CARNIVAL.

Here, also, this little episode gains undoubtedly in clearness, if its dual rhythm is understood, and the accents given accordingly.

SCHUMANN—GRILLEN.

Schumann's Notation.

Altered Notation.

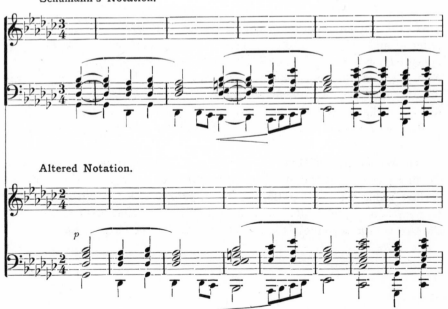

In the altered notation I have changed the triple into dual time, in order to make rhythm and time agree. The syncopated phrases have disappeared, having been moved back into their natural position. The movement, through this replacement, begins with the full measure, and all the phrases and accents become positive. The interpretation is thus quite plain, and the composer's ideas, instead of suffering by this treatment, have really been more faithfully portrayed than by following his own whimsical indication.

The second part of this movement requires unravelling even more than the first part; and I therefore give it in full in its altered notation, without further remark, excepting the advice to compare this notation with the original one. The student will draw his own conclusion as to which of the two notations conveys the composer's idea in the clearest manner.

SCHUMANN—Grillen.

THIRD PHASE OF NEGATIVE ACCENTS.

The prescribed time being entirely antagonistic to the actual rhythm.

Great latitude is allowed to every composer; he is not to be dictated
to, or curbed in his flight of fancy. But when it comes to the mere
mechanical part—notation, the composer is as much bound to adhere to
grammatical rules, as the prose-writer or poet is obliged to observe correct
spelling and punctuation.

Let a composer write as many dissonances as he pleases, change his
rhythm as often as he likes, let him introduce confusing rhythmical
episodes, and adhere during these episodes to the general time; but, to
write a whole movement in antagonistic time, this is stepping beyond the
latitude allowed to a composer. This is a mannerism, a fault, for which
Schumann has often and justly been blamed; for example:

SCHUMANN—Des Abends, Op. 12, No. 1.

One can really not help wondering, why Schumann prescribed here
double ($\frac{2}{8}$) time, when throughout the piece the movement is unquestionably in triple ($\frac{3}{8}$) time.

Was it to mystify the student, or to enhance the beauty of the
work?

If so, he certainly succeeded in the former, but failed in the latter.

Let the student simply consider the whole piece to be in ($\frac{3}{8}$) time,
and it will all be plain sailing.

Apropos of this kind of anomaly, Tschaïkowsky, the clever and
spirituel Russian composer, has launched a humorous shaft against Schumann, by giving in his "Theme originale et Variations," Op. 19, the following absurd time-indication to one of the variations.

P. TSCHAÏKOWSKY, Op. 19.   VAR. XI.—*Alla* SCHUMANN.

Allegro brillante.

etc.

The notation of $\frac{3}{4}$ time is, of course, absurd, since the measure contains only two quarters.

This is by no means an engraver's fault, or an oversight of the proofreader. It must be taken as illustrating Tschaïkowsky's sarcasm upon similar cases, almost as absurd, and occurring in Schumann's works; hence, the heading of the variation, "*Alla* Schumann."

But Schumann does not stand alone in committing this kind of abnormity. I shall cite two cases of Chopin, in which the prescribed time is opposed to the rhythm of an entire movement.

First example:

CHOPIN—ETUDE, Op. 25, No. 2.

Chopin's Notation.

Presto.

p   molto legato.

etc.

In this well-known etude, either the accents are wrong when given in accordance with the prescribed time, or the alla brève time is wrong when the accents are given in accordance with the rhythm.

Compare the following notation:

Altered Notation.

Presto.

p

etc.

molto legato.

This change of time is always made by every one who plays the etude correctly, perhaps made unconsciously ; but the fact remains the same.

The rhythm is the chief carrier of the composer's idea, and cannot be changed without impairing that idea.

The grammatical accents, which follow the rhythm, cannot be changed either.

If, therefore, time and rhythm, or time and rhythmical accents, do not agree—as in the above case—it must be the time which is wrong. It may, in fact, be laid down as a general principle, that

It is always the rhythm that decides the time, and not the time which prescribes the rhythm.

As a proof that Chopin's alla brève time (¢) was incorrect, and misleading, observe that his triplets would have to be accented thus :

Compare, for example, the accents of Etude No. 8, same opus,

Both kinds of triplets are accented alike, but neither would be in accordance with the proper rhythm of the F-minor Etude (No. 2).

Had Chopin written sextuplets, instead of triplets, it would have been better; for example :

but the plainest and clearest notation is always that of writing the whole etude in $\frac{6}{8}$ time :

Second example:

CHOPIN—Prelude, Op. 28, No. 1.

Chopin's Notation.

etc.

This prelude is another glaring instance of negative accents caused by antagonistic time-indication.

On account of the time being unsound from the outset, the rhythmical notation is unnecessarily complicated, the melody obscured, the accents removed, and the reader mystified. As a result, this prelude is rarely quite understood, or correctly interpreted.

The nature of the rhythm demanded that this prelude should have been written in triple, not in dual time, and more especially, in $\frac{3}{8}$ time. This would have changed the negative into positive accents, thrown the melody into plainly perceptible relief, and caused the accents to fall conspicuously, yet naturally, upon the ear, without in the least degree altering the intended effect.

As the prelude is short, I subjoin it here entirely in its natural notation.

CHOPIN—Prelude, Op. 28, No. 1.

Altered Notation.
Agitato.

A composer may succeed in deceiving the reader's eye, but he cannot deceive the listener's ear. Accents on a melody so plain as in this prelude will naturally assert themselves, and fall together with the strong part of the time, in spite of antagonistic notation.

One more example of this awkward and confusing kind of notation. Every pianist is supposed to know Schumann's beautiful A-minor Concerto, although not every one may have studied it. Those who have done so, and have attended its rehearsals with orchestra, may have been sensible of a certain feeling of apprehension on the approach of the syncopated part of the last movement, which is the subject of the next example.

SCHUMANN—Concerto in A-Minor, Op. 54.

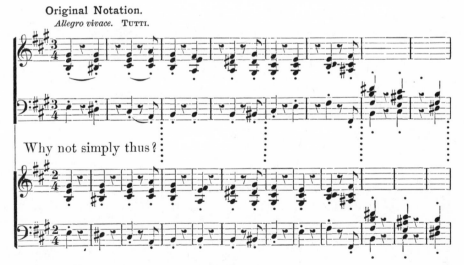

The awkwardness of this movement is caused by the composer trying to force a double rhythm upon triple time. If this movement were merely a short episode, the adherence to the general time ($\frac{3}{4}$) might be excusable, but since it is the second subject of the finale, and consists of forty measures, it is not an episode, and the persistence in the general time is hardly justified.

It might be observed, in defence of such rhythmical wilfulness, that those who attempt to play this concerto ought to be such good musicians as fully to comprehend the dual character of the rhythm, without being led astray by the triple time. Yet this is no reason why the notation should not be made as plain as possible, especially as it is so easy a matter; while, as the notation stands, experience proves that even the best-trained orchestra and conductor come generally to some hitch during rehearsals.

A simple remedy would be to contract every two measures, containing together six quarters, into one measure of $\frac{3}{2}$ time; for example:

Or, still better, that the entire movement of forty measures be written in $\frac{2}{4}$ time; thus:

This would bring the time in accordance with the rhythm, obviate all awkwardness, and still convey faithfully the composer's ideas.

The piano solo would appear thus:

And finish in this way:

CHAPTER III.

CHARACTERISTIC ACCENTS.

ALMOST every civilized country has its national melodies, in the form of songs, dances, or marches. While most of these melodies have remained local, some of them, particularly dances, have been taken up by the great masters and introduced into general musical literature; and though many of the original melodies have long been forgotten, or changed, yet the form and characteristic elements of them have remained.

The most notable traits of these tunes are the rhythm and a peculiar accentuation by which certain characteristic points of the rhythm are made prominent.

As it is the above accents which bring out such rhythmical points, the name given to them seems appropriate.

They impart to the melodies that characteristic element which, though it cannot be called foreign, because music is a cosmopolitan language belonging to all nations, yet is so distinctly national, as to enable any one familiar with the characteristics of such airs to recognize readily the nationality to which they belong.

Characteristic accents are exclusively rhythmical, but cannot be translated, so to speak, into grammatical accents, because they mark the rhythm in their own peculiar manner, independent of strong and weak time-parts; and we accept them intact, as we accept a foreign phrase, which we should only spoil by translation.

Therefore, characteristic accents should be considered as independent rhythmical ones, apart from grammatical rules, and dependent only on the rhythmical characteristics of national tunes, generally dances, which it is their object to portray.

But there is also another kind of characteristic accent, similar to the former in its independence and disregard of grammatical rules, but differing from the former in so much as, instead of portraying the rhythmical characteristics of national tunes, it portrays the individual vein of the composer. The former we will call *positive;* the latter, *individual.*

a. Positive Characteristic Accents.

These portray something positive in rhythmical characteristics, something national, historical, the omitting or altering of which would impair the character, and, with it, the nationality.

For instance: The accents of a waltz, belonging to that undulating kind of movement peculiar to the German waltz, if omitted or altered, would injure its character.

The accents of a mazurka, belonging to the characteristic step or foot-stamping peculiar to that Polish dance, if omitted or altered, would weaken the character of the mazurka.

As so it is with the accents of every national dance.

A dance depends upon certain turns of the body. Each turn constituting a *pas;* each *pas* being determined by a step, a down-coming of the body, or we might say, by a *corporal* accent. It is only natural, that in the accompanying music each corporal accent should be indicated by a corresponding musical accent. We may thus conclude that to every musical accent belongs an accent of the body, or, *vice versa,* to every corporeal accent a musical one. And further, that, if this law is not observed, the music and the dance-steps are not together, not in time.*

---

* Believing it to be an appropriate quotation, I give here the remarks which Charles Reade makes in his novel, "Christie Johnstone," in reference to reel-dancing. "The principle of reel-dancing is articulation ; the foot strikes the ground for every *accented* note (and, by the bye, it is their weakness of accent which makes all English reel and hornpipe playing such failures), and in the best steps of all, which it has in common with the hornpipe, such as the quick "heel and toe," the "sailor's fling," and the "double shuffle," the foot strikes the ground for every *single* note of the instrument.".... "Articulate dancing, compared with the loose, lawless diffluence of motion that goes by the name of dancing,

The great masters who employed certain national dance-forms for special compositions, or introduced them in their greater works, although describing the general distinctions of these dances, did not adhere strictly enough to the more detailed characteristics; and handled the *form* with such individual freedom, that it became under their hands an *artistic dance-form,* but ceased to be a dance in the popular acceptation.

Thus, the dances of Bach; the minuets of Haydn, Mozart, and Beethoven; the waltzes and polonaises of Schubert; the mazurkas, waltzes, and polonaises of Chopin, etc., are artistic forms; and not intended for practical dance purposes. They are poetized, idealized dances for the artistic taste; very different from the dances of Strauss, Lanner, Labitzki, Gungl, etc., which are for the enjoyment of the masses.

It is not necessary to examine here the characteristics of every country's national music; a few examples, however, of the dance-forms most frequently met with in pianoforte music may be of interest, and convey the idea of positive characteristic accents.

The positive characteristic accents of a *mazurka* are these:

falling on the first and third beat; and, at the end of a phrase or period, on the first and second beat.

The variations of this formula—which are to be found in great number in Chopin's mazurkas—are always based upon this general idea, viz.: of accenting the first and third beat, and, periodically, the second beat. When these variations do not alter the rhythm too much, they do not materially weaken the character of the mazurka.

The accents of a *polka* are:

two in each measure, on the first and second beat; while the end of a phrase or period has three accents, as in the above formula.

---

gives me (I must confess) as much more pleasure, as the clean playing of my mother to the pianoforte splashing of my daughter; though the latter does attack the instrument as a washer-woman her soap suds, and the former works like a lady.....What says Goldsmith of the two styles? 'They swam, sprawled, frisked, and languished ; but Olivia's foot was as pat to the music as its echo.' "

The accents of a polka would almost be grammatical, if the measure were $\frac{4}{8}$, instead of $\frac{2}{4}$, which accounts for the resemblance between a polka and a quick-march, and explains why in Austrian military bands a polka is often played instead of a march, and a march instead of a polka.

The *polonaise* is a kind of stately march, or promenade; not a dance, strictly speaking. Although written in $\frac{3}{4}$ time, the movement is in eighths; not, however, in $\frac{6}{8}$, the multiple of twice three, with two accents, but as multiple of three times two, with three accents.

The rhythm of the accompaniment is this:

with this occasional change,

The accents of the polonaise melody are very characteristic; for example:

falling, as a rule, on the first and second eighths in the first measure, and on the first and second quarters in the second measure. This form of accentuation is repeated, or slightly altered, in successive phrases; and the end of a period, or part, has this almost invariable phrase:

instead of,

These characteristic endings formerly accompanied a stately bow of the partners to each other, as in the well known-figure of the Lancers.

The *bolero*, originally a Spanish song, with pantomimic gestures, became a dance accompanied by castanets, guitar, or tambourine.

The rhythm of the castanets:

or,

resembles the polonaise accompaniment.

Another resemblance to the polonaise is the prevalence of eighths ($\frac{1}{8}$) in the movement, and also the syncopic accent on the second eighth in the first measure of a phrase or period. The general accents are these:

But, notwithstanding the resemblance in rhythm, accentuation, and tempo, there are yet unmistakable distinctions between these two dances. For example, when a polonaise has this figure:

the bolero has this one:

The sharp points in the rhythm of the polonaise give to it a stateliness, a certain nobleness, which the bolero lacks; instead of which, the bolero, by greater employment of triplets, has more animation and a kind of roundness, which the polonaise has not.

The movements and gestures of the dancers are graceful and subtle, neither stately, as in the polonaise, nor excited, as in the Italian tarantella.

HUNGARIAN MUSIC

represents three distinct elements:

1. The heroic-patriotic; as in their marches and martial music.
2. The nomadic, wild, untamed; as in their dances and gipsy music.
3. And lastly, the sad and wailful; as in their songs.

These elements are so strangely intermingled by surprising changes in tempo, in rhythm, and accentuation, that the chief characteristics in the movements of their music—more characteristic even than the harmonic changes—is an almost constant rubato, an alternate change of extremes in tempo, of retardation and acceleration, which, in most cases, is brought to an end by the following characteristic phrase:

mostly in slow, retarding tempo, but also in quick tempo without retarda-

7

tion; for example, in Brahms's "Hungarian Dances." The following peculiar rhythm occurs frequently in their music :

or this syncopated rhythm :

(See Brahms's "Hungarian Dances.")

There is nothing very characteristic in English national music.

Scotch national music, however, is more interesting, being rich in beautiful songs, and in lively and spirited dances and marches.

The following figure frequently occurs in their rhythm :

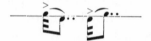

and is their chief rhythmical characteristic.

All their real national tunes lack the interval of the fourth and seventh, which are frequently wanting even in more modern Scotch songs and dances. This fact is evidently owing to the incomplete scale of the old bagpipes, which had only these notes: *g a b d e g* (wanting the *c*, and *f♯*).

It is a strange coincidence, that in the national music of the western part of Europe the rhythm and accentuation are more steady and regular than in the eastern part, where they are more nervous, almost spasmodic.

The most numerous and fanciful accentuation is probably to be met with in the music of the Slavonic races, notably the Polish and Russian; and the most fanciful rhythm is to be found in Hungarian music.

Attempting a comparison, in rhythmical respect, between the music of the German and the Slavonic races, we would find the following distinction :

German rhythm, as a rule, begins quietly and increases in animation; for example :

Slavonic rhythm, in direct opposition, starts in full animation and then decreases in speed; for example:

This is not an occasional, but a fundamental distinction in the character as well as the music of these races.

The Germans, being phlegmatic, require time and rousing to get *en train;* the Slavs, being impulsive and impetuous, begin in full swing, and soon subside.

Believing that I have sufficiently explained, although in a rather sketchy way, what is to be understood by "characteristic accents" in general, and by positive ones in particular, I now turn to those accents which vary from, or go beyond, the positive ones, and belong to the individuality of the composer, frequently arising out of his nationality.

Many of Chopin's accents, for example, bear the stamp of, and arise out of, his nationality; while Schumann's accents are characteristic only in being whimsical, syncopic, negative, but have nothing national in them.

b. Individual Characteristic Accents.

Musical art recognizes two kinds of music—artistic music, the production of the artist,—and national music, the production of the people.

If we liken music to flowers, the former would be the cultivated, and the latter the wild flowers. A third kind of music, appropriately called "trash," provided by publishers, and consumed by that portion of the public, which, not unlike certain long-eared animals, prefers thistles to roses, is not recognized, and might be likened to the weeds, which it ought to be the duty of every artist to uproot.

Artistic music accepts and amalgamates in itself the contributions and productions of every country, and therefore, having neither geographical boundaries nor any particular nationality, is universal, cosmopolitan.

National music, however, being the music of the people, associated with their traditions, habits, and peculiarities, is local, characteristic to a particular race, and more a thing of the past than of the present.

It does not matter to what nationality a musician belongs, if only he has passed through the same studies of the great masters and is working with the same object as all, to attain the highest perfection in and for his art; he is then entitled to be a member of the universal brotherhood of musical artists.

But if an artist (here, more particularly, a composer) retains the characteristics of his nationality beyond a certain degree, he cannot avoid—unless he has rare originality and genius—remaining one-sided, according to the catholicity of musical art. Therefore, a creative musician must, to a certain extent, renounce or lose his nationality, and have no exclusive predilection for one style of compositions. But the intuitive power of genius is always an exception to every rule.

With Chopin, for instance, this one-sidedness was his greatest charm. His unquestioned genius was always original; his creations, although limited to the pianoforte, and bearing the stamp more of a particular than a cosmopolitan character, marked nevertheless a new era in pianoforte-playing, and had a powerful influence on the progress of music in general.

Now, to interpret correctly any musical work of a strictly national character, it is first necessary to be acquainted with the salient characteristics of such country's national music, in order to separate what is really national from what is the outgrowth of the composer's personality.

For instance, in Liszt's Hungarian rhapsodies, in Chopin's Polish dances, in Tschaïkowsky's Russian, or Grieg's Scandinavian melodies, in the numerous Spanish and Italian serenades, barcarolles, etc., there is to be found a certain positive national element around which each composer has woven his own personality.

Although it may not be difficult to perceive the difference between negative grammatical and characteristic accents, it is not so easy to distinguish between what belongs to positive and what to individual characteristics.

A few illustrations will, however, better explain this difference than any lengthened discourse.

CHOPIN—Valse, Op. 64, No. 2.

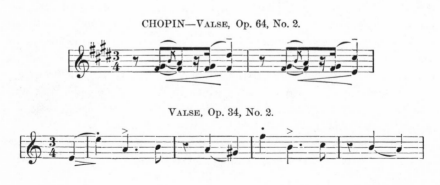

Valse, Op. 34, No. 2.

VALSE, Op. 64, No. 3.

VALSE, Op. posthumous, No. 4.

Chopin's accents bear here unmistakably the stamp of the Polish mazurka, rather than of the German waltz; the Slavonic element oozing out, so to say, of every pore. These waltzes cannot be called German.

CHOPIN—POLONAISE, Op. 53.

THE SAME OPUS.

POLONAISE, Op. 22.

Who ever, before Chopin, conceived such extraordinary rhythm and rhythmical accentuation as are shown in these polonaises? And yet, one feels that Chopin is here at home.

After having become familiar with his personality, all becomes quite natural and easy-flowing, because there is nothing labored or made up; even in his most complicated abandon the ideas are born ready-made, and entirely free from conventionalism.

CHOPIN—Krakowiak, Op. 14.

Rondo, Op. 1.   Rondo, Op. 16.

Inasmuch as characteristic accents are altogether irregular and uncertain, the whole subject has necessarily been treated in only a very general and imperfect way.

The positive accents of this class permitted merely the mentioning of certain rhythmical peculiarities, essential to particular national tunes; while the individual accents of this class, more irregular and spontaneous than the former, were quite beyond the control of reasoning.

But though it is impossible to lay down any regulation of these accents, from a rhythmical point of view, we are yet able to systematize their observance from a melodic aspect, as will be seen subsequently.

In fact, characteristic accents will receive a far more detailed analysis melodically, than it is possible to give them rhythmically.

PART II.

METRICAL ACCENTS.

WHILE the previous rhythmical accents corresponded, in language, to syllabic accentuation, the present metrical ones correspond to the emphasis which is laid upon one word of a sentence to make that word prominent.

" *If accent is syllabic emphasis, emphasis is logical accent.*"

As the emphasis which is given to a word will naturally fall together with the accent given to a syllable, so does metrical emphasis, which is given to the beginning of a measure, fall together with rhythmic accent given to the primary strong part of a measure.

But, as the former is the more important, it has precedence over the latter, on the simple principle that a stronger accent always dominates a weaker one and causes the latter to recede.

Metrical accents have this in common with rhythmical ones, that, like the latter, they are governed by the grammatical rules of accenting the strong and not accenting the weak parts ; which rule includes the principle, that two strong parts should not follow each other, without one or two weak ones coming in between them.

On the other hand, metrical accents differ from rhythmical ones in this : Whereas the latter affect the rhythmic motion by giving a clear sense of its details, metrical accents affect the metrical formation by giving prominence to the musical parts of speech, called :

SECTION ; PHRASE ; PERIOD ;

which, in punctuation, would require a comma (**,**) a semicolon (**;**) or a full stop (**.**).

Because metrical accents fall invariably and only on the beginning of measures, they are frequently confounded with the so-called " measure-

[*Germ.* 'Tact'] accents;" and, *vice versa*, the accents denoting the measure are confounded with metrical accents.

It is not difficult to show how inexact such misconception is. For example, supposing this thesis were advanced: to denote a measure, *the beginning of the measure* should be accented.

Would this thesis be correct? Could it be logically maintained in accordance with grammatical rule?

I say, no!

If we denoted a measure by accenting its beginning, then, to denote the next measure, we should have to accent the beginning of that also, and so on with all succeeding measures.

But, by so doing, we would not observe grammatical principles, according to which two accents should not follow each other, without one or two weak parts falling between them. Hence, after an accented measure should follow one or two unaccented ones.

Therefore, the above thesis cannot be logically maintained, and ought to be modified as follows:

To denote a measure, *the strong part of it* should be accented.

This is far from being merely a petty distinction, for it involves an important principle.

By accenting the strong time-part of a measure (which falls on the beginning), we denote the *measure*.

By emphasizing the beginning of a measure, we mark the measure as the strong part of the two (or three) measures, hence we denote *a section*.

By emphasizing the beginning of a section, we mark the section as the strong part of two (or three) sections, hence we denote *a phrase*.

By emphasizing the beginning of a phrase, we mark the phrase as the strong part of two (or three) phrases, hence we denote a *period*.

And yet, it is evident that, in denoting a period, a phrase, a section, or a single measure, the accent falls always on the primary strong part of a measure, virtually a rhythmical part.

CHAPTER IV.

METRICAL FORMATION.—GENERAL FACTS AND RULES.

METRICAL formation has two extremes—the measure, and the period.

The former is the unit, the material of which the latter is constructed; the latter is the aim and end of metrical formation, as a sentence is the aim and end of grammatical formation in language.

A musical composition is made up of periods, as a literary work is made up of sentences; one period or sentence succeeding another.

Metrical accentuation throws these periods as well as their parts, the phrases and sections, into relief, by proportionate emphasis; and separates all these time-groups by breaks, as the parts of sentences are separated by punctuation.

This accenting and dividing depends, however, entirely on the performer's discernment of the different time-groups, viz.: on their exact terminations; for, *to terminate a group*, is *to discern it*.

But we cannot terminate a group correctly, unless we know its necessary and permissible extent, viz.: the smallest and largest number of measures which limit a group.

It is, therefore, necessary to examine the material, the formation and extent of every kind of metrical group, in order to arrive at the faculty of terminating, *i. e.*, discerning any section, phrase, and period.

A measure, as the unit of metrical groups, must be intact.

Hence, all metrical groups, whether section, phrase, or period, contain full measures.

When, therefore, a period commences with only part of a measure (which it may do), it must end with the corresponding part to make up the incomplete beginning.

A measure, in musical *architectonic*, might thus be likened to a stone, in the construction of a building, both representing the unit of a uniform material. If a row begin with half a stone, or a period with half a measure, both should end with the other half, to complete a perfect row, or a perfect period.

It may also be observed, that the beginning of the musical subject contained in the first measure determines the beginning of all the succeeding groups (sections, phrases, periods,) until the end of a movement is reached. For, on whatever time-part the subject begins, all the metrical groups following begin with the same, and end with the corresponding time-part.

Metrical accents emphasize the beginning of measures only, and not the beginning of any time-group commencing with an incomplete measure.

Metrical groups commencing with a full measure are said to have a strong beginning; and those commencing with an incomplete measure, a weak beginning.

The endings, also, are either strong or weak, according to the time-parts they fall on.

A period has, as a rule, eight measures, four sections, two phrases. This is the most rational, and by far the most frequently employed formation.

Many theorists consider the eight-measured period and melody as the natural and normal basis of perfect musical form, while others hold the four-measured phrase to be the ground-form of musical construction.

Lobe, being of the former opinion, goes even further; for he finds in the eight-measured period and melody "the nucleus around which is woven the whole technical work of tonic, harmonic, rhythmic, metric, and thematic construction, the chief point from which emerges all this technical work."—(I. C. Lobe, *Compositions-Lehre, Weimar,* 1844.)

We, for our part, shall consider the eight-measured period containing four sections, and two phrases, as the normal and positive one; and all other periods, extended beyond the number of eight measures, as abnormal and negative. We shall not recognize a group of less than eight measures as a period at all; for a period should have at least two phrases; a phrase, two sections; a section, two measures. A group of six or seven measures, therefore, is only a phrase.

In this view, the eight-measured period is a metrical consonance, as the positive grammatical accents are rhythmical consonances; and all other periods are metrical dissonances, as the negative rhythmical accents are rhythmical dissonances.

The metrical dissonances of irregular periods, however, are by no means objectionable, but, on the contrary, are quite as logical and necessary as other dissonances.

Metrical accentuation, like phrasing, depends entirely, as has already been said, on the performer's consciousness of the formation and extent of metrical groups.

When these groups are symmetrical, having the normal number of measures, they are readily perceived, and accentuation is exceedingly simple. But, when these groups are not symmetrical, having an irregular number of measures, they are sometimes difficult to discern, and render metrical phrasing by no means easy.

Regular periods and their accents are so very simple, that one or two examples will be all that is needed.

We shall not, however, get over the irregular periods quite so easily.

a. Regular Periods.

The following example illustrates an eight-measured period beginning with a full measure.

SCHUMANN—ARABESQUE, Op. 18.

The accent denoting the period is naturally the strongest.

The accents marking the phrases are of secondary grade, and those marking the sections are of tertiary grade.

This arrangement accords with grammatical principles, and corresponds exactly to the grading of rhythmical accents.

EXAMPLE.

Grading of Metrical Accents in an Eight-measured Period.

I.		II.		III.		IV.	
∧			PERIOD.				
	PHRASE.			∧		PHRASE.	
Section.		∧	Section.		Section.	∧	Section.
1	2	3	4	5	6	7	8

Grading of Rhythmical Accents in One Measure.

The fact, that the accent on the first measure of the period is metrically the strongest one, does not exclude the admission of still stronger accents on other parts of the period; for, by the same reasoning by which a secondary accent recedes before a primary one, or a tertiary before a secondary one, the strongest metrical accent may have to recede before a still stronger melodic one.

(See Schumann's accents, in the previous example, second, fourth, sixth, and eighth measures.)

The next example illustrates a regular period beginning with a weak time-part, called an "up-beat" (Germ. "Auftakt"); in prosody, "*thesis.*"

BEETHOVEN—SONATA, Op. 31, No. 3.

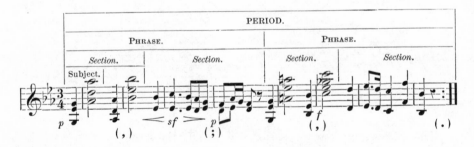

The subject represents here, rhythmically, a musical *iambus*, (= ‿ —), and care should be taken that this tact-foot is not accented like a trochee, (— ‿), which is just the opposite. *Apropos* of these two opposite tact-feet, I would call attention to the following episode in Schumann's " Faschingsschwank," Op. 26 :

The composer, having chosen this iambus as his rhythmical subject, repeats this tact-foot without intermission, or rhythmical change, during forty-eight measures, and, moreover, without becoming monotonous.

His method of indicating the accentuation being an unusual one, therefore occasionally found fault with, is, nevertheless, not only quite correct, but deserving even of especial notice; for by no other means of notation could the performer so forcibly be reminded of bringing out the iambus,

and of avoiding the trochee,

than by Schumann's way of slurring (♪ ♪ | ♩) the two notes.

The performer, though comprehending these indications, may yet be puzzled how to avoid the trochee; because the latter will assert itself spontaneously to the ear, although the opposite effect is aimed at, especially in instances where the iambic foot is repeated for any length of time. The only remedy, in such cases, is the due observance of that important rule of phrasing which demands that *the last note of any slurred group shall be shortened to about one-half of its value,* in order to produce a break, a termination.

According to this rule, all iambic tact-feet—for example, the subject of Beethoven's period—should be rendered in this way:

and the iambus will then fall unmistakably upon the ear.

The punctuation, which was attached to both the previous examples of periods, indicated the incisions, or *cæsuræ*, of the period; which terms signify the natural pause or rest of the voice, where breath may be taken, in speaking or singing, and the hand raised out of position in pianoforte-playing.

Correct observance of these incisions or breaks is of the greatest moment in musical phrasing. In fact, phrasing chiefly depends on them; because they effect a termination, and, by thus separating the phrase from the next one, throw it into relief even more effectively than the accent on the beginning of the phrase alone could do.

b. Irregular Periods.

Metrical formation (counting upward from the measure to the period) or metrical division (counting downward from the period to the measure) has this in common with rhythmical division, that, like the latter, *it is either double or triple.**

In other words: A Period has either two or three Phrases.
              A Phrase has either two or three Sections.
              A Section has either two or three Measures.
              A Measure, as a unit, must be intact.

Hence arise many combinations as to the number of measures of which metrical time-groups may be formed; for example:

A *Section* may have two Measures or three Measures, giving two kinds of Sections.

A *Phrase* may have

    1. *Two* Sections of   2 and 2 = 4 Measures,
    2.   "   "   2 and 3 = 5   "
    3.   "   "   3 and 2 = 5   "
    4.   "   "   3 and 3 = 6   "
    5. Or *three* Sections of 2, 2 and 2 = 6 Measures,
    6.   "   "   2, 2 and 3 = 7   "
    7.   "   "   2, 3 and 2 = 7   "
    8.   "   "   2, 3 and 3 = 8   "

---

* Though simple and irrefragable, this theory has, to the author's knowledge, never yet been brought forward.

9. *Three* Sections of 3, 2 and 2 = 7 Measures,
10. "   "   3, 2 and 3 = 8   "
11. "   "   3, 3 and 2 = 8   "
12. "   "   3, 3 and 3 = 9   "

giving twelve kinds of Phrases.

A Period may have two Phrases in 12 times 12 = 144 combinations, or three Phrases in 12 times 144 = 1728 combinations, giving a total of 1872 kinds of Periods.*

These numerous combinations result in this:

The Subject has always 1 Measure.
The smallest Section has 2 Measures, the largest has 3 Measures.
The   "   Phrase   4   "   the   "   " 9   "
The   "   Period   8   "   the   "   " 27   "

All these combinations are theoretically and mathematically correct, and as possible as the carrying on of scales up to twelve sharps and twelve flats. Although many of the long periods are not actually employed, yet they are a great deal more feasible than scales with eight, nine, or more accidentals.

Why should not a musical period of the longest possible extent be employed under some peculiar circumstance, just as well as excessively long sentences, inasmuch as such a period might serve some bizarre purpose or odd

---

* A *Period of two Phrases* may be constructed of

Phrases 1 and 1,	Phrases 2 and 1,	Phrases 3 and 1,
" 1 and 2,	" 2 and 2,	" 3 and 2,
" 1 and 3,	" 2 and 3,	" 3 and 3,
and so on to	and so on to	and so on to
Phrases 1 and 12,	Phrases 2 and 12,	Phrases 3 and 12,
giving 1 × 12 = 12 Periods.	giving 2 × 12 = 24 Periods.	giving 3 × 12 = 36 Phrases.

And so on to 12 × 12 = 144 Periods of two Phrases.

A *Period of three Phrases* may be constructed of

Phrase 1 and any one of the above 144 Periods,
"   2   "   "   "   "
"   3   "   "   "   "   and so on to
"   12   "   "   "   "

giving 12 times 144 or 1728 Periods of three Phrases.
Add to this, 144 Periods of two Phrases.

Total,   1872 Periods.

whim of the composer; for example, the spinning-out of the period might be intended to represent the prolonged agony of the never-dying primo tenore, in Italian opera, or the tantalizing effect of the withheld ending might have some reason as ingenious as that of an eccentric composer, of my acquaintance, who, in his "Grande Symphonie Infernale," made all the instruments descend in consecutive perfect fifths down to the lowest depth, in order to portray the howling and infernal discord of the damned, who were hungry and wanted something to eat.

Excessively long periods are certainly not beautiful, but are, nevertheless, quite as permissible as the above intentionally spun-out sentence. Without advocating the employment of either, the right of existence may be conceded to both.

Leaving aside theoretical periods of extreme length, and taking into consideration actually employed ones only, it is difficult, without searching the entire range of pianoforte-literature, to state with absolute certainty, up to what length irregular periods have really been used.

Periods of nine, ten, eleven, and twelve measures occur frequently. Also those up to thirteen, fourteen, and fifteen measures; but here they generally stop.

Although I do not say that larger periods are not to be met with, yet, as a rule, I am pretty safe in limiting the extent of generally employed phrases to seven, and of periods to fifteen measures.

Practical illustrations being usually more instructive, and having quicker results than long dissertations, I shall give some examples of regular and irregular periods, from the works of Chopin and Beethoven. These will cover all requirements.

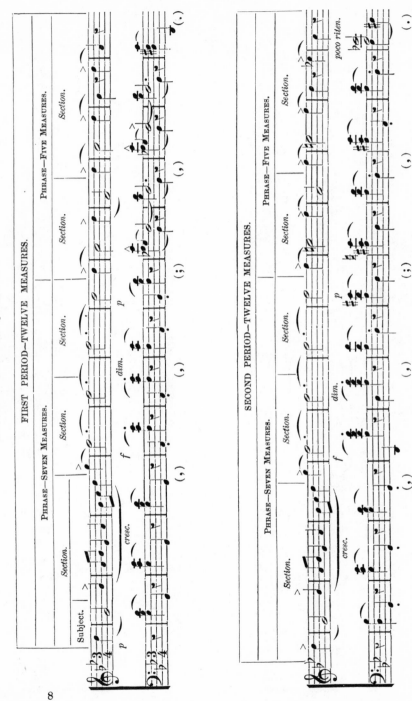

CHOPIN—Nocturne, Op. 15, No. 3.

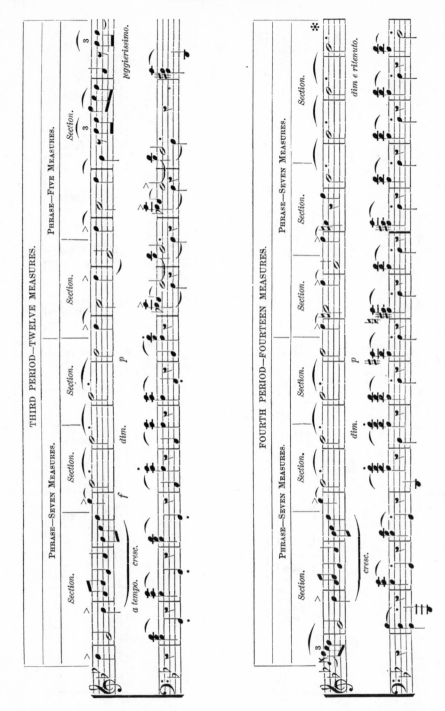

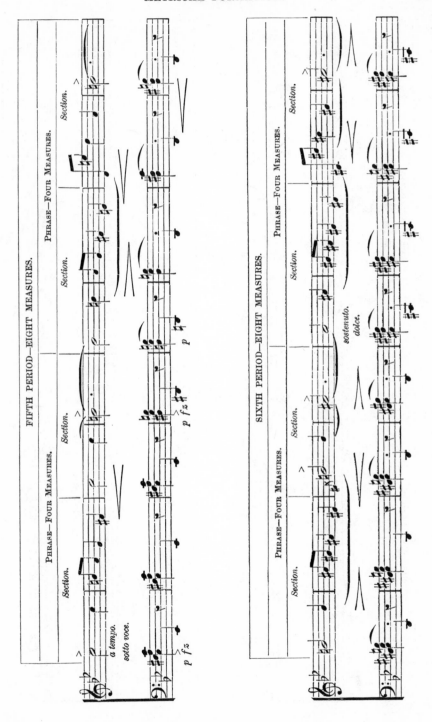

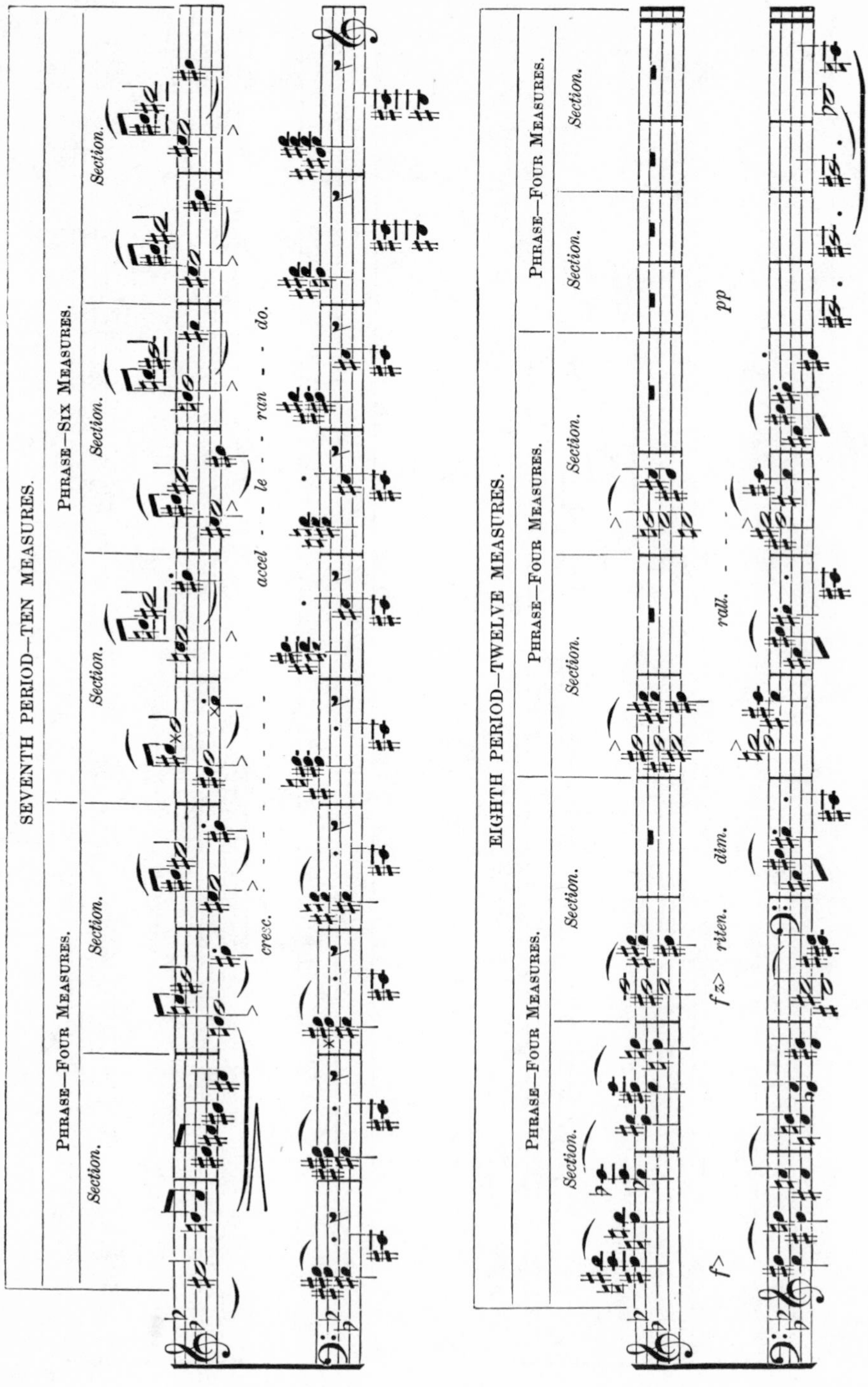
SEVENTH PERIOD—TEN MEASURES.
PHRASE—FOUR MEASURES.
PHRASE—SIX MEASURES.
Section.
Section.
Section.
Section.
Section.
cresc.
accel - - le - - ran - - do.
EIGHTH PERIOD—TWELVE MEASURES.
PHRASE—FOUR MEASURES.
PHRASE—FOUR MEASURES.
PHRASE—FOUR MEASURES.
Section.
Section.
Section.
Section.
Section.
Section.
f>
fz>
riten.
dim.
rall.
pp

From this point, the second part begins. This it is unnecessary to review, as it contains only regular periods.

The asterisk, ✻, at the last measure of the fourth period, calls attention to an irregularity of metrical measurement.

Chopin here follows the precepts of Beethoven and other great masters, who, when it suits their purpose, occasionally add, or take off, a fractional part at the end of a period, in order to commence the succeeding periods with a strong beginning, when the previous periods had commenced with a weak one, or *vice versa*.

The most appropriate term for designating the metrical work of analyzing and dividing a composition into periods, phrases, and sections, would be the word *periodizing*.

Periodizing is one of the most important aids in comprehending and interpreting a composition. Being an intellectual acquirement, entirely independent of emotion or taste, it can be subjected to precise principles and rules.

The first step in periodizing a composition is to ascertain where each period ends.

FIRST RULE.

The termination of a period is shown by the reappearance of the old, or the commencement of a new subject; because, with the reappearance of the old, or the commencement of a new subject, another period begins.

By examining the periods of Chopin's nocturne, it will be found that the termination of the first six periods was determined by the symmetrical reappearance of the original subject; and the termination of the seventh and eighth periods, by the commencement of new subjects.

The next step is to ascertain the termination of phrases and sections.

The rule just given is here equally applicable.

The termination of either phrase or section is likewise to be ascertained by a symmetrical beginning of the next one, or through quite a new beginning.

SECOND RULE.

Each metrical group should be as much as possible a unit in itself. Periodizing should respect this unity, and not cut into it.

The consideration of such unity is of decisive importance when any doubt arises as to whether

A Section has 2 or 3 Measures,
A Phrase has 2 or 3 Sections, or
A Period has 2 or 3 Phrases;

for example: where two sections have five measures, or three sections have seven measures, and it is doubtful to which of the sections the odd number of measures belong; or, where two phrases have five sections, or three phrases have seven sections, and it is doubtful to which of the phrases the odd number of sections belong, etc.

Compare now the sections and phrases in our illustration, and ascertain whether there is such unity in them.

By examining the first period of Chopin's nocturne, we find that it terminated with the twelfth measure, because the original subject reappeared in the thirteenth measure. This gave us a period of twelve measures.

The first phrase terminated at the seventh measure, by a symmetrical appearance of the subject in the eighth measure. This gave us two phrases, of seven and five measures respectively.

The first section was terminated with the third instead of the second measure, by the evident unity of the second and third measures which could not be disjoined.

The second, third, and fourth sections had plainly two measures each.

The last section, with three measures, had evidently more right to them, on account of greater unity, than the fourth section.

This gives us five sections, of three, two, two, two, and three measures respectively.

If the student will now examine the other periods in the same way, he will find these rules equally observed, and applicable as well as adequate for all similar metrical work.

As a second illustration, I choose the *allegro* of Beethoven's First Sonata; one of the simplest in form, and composed in his earlier style, while yet under the influence of Haydn and Mozart.

The *allegro* begins with an incomplete measure. We may begin the periods from the incomplete beginning, as we have done before, or from the full measure, as is generally done. Both ways answer the same purpose.

Having before commenced with the incomplete measure, we shall now try the other way.

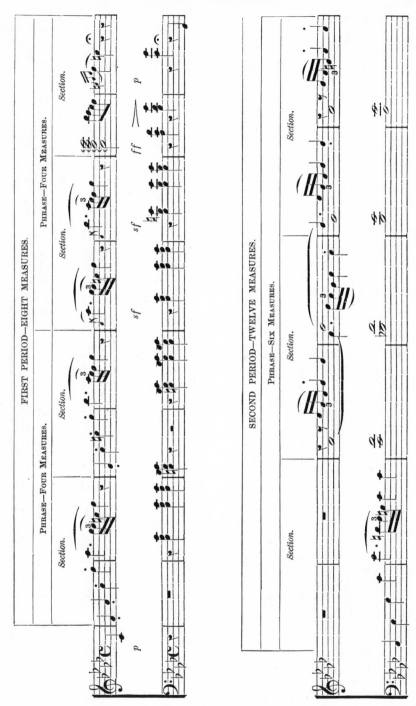

BEETHOVEN—Sonata, Op. 2, No. 1.

FIRST PERIOD—EIGHT MEASURES.

PHRASE—FOUR MEASURES.

PHRASE—FOUR MEASURES.

SECOND PERIOD—TWELVE MEASURES.

PHRASE—SIX MEASURES.

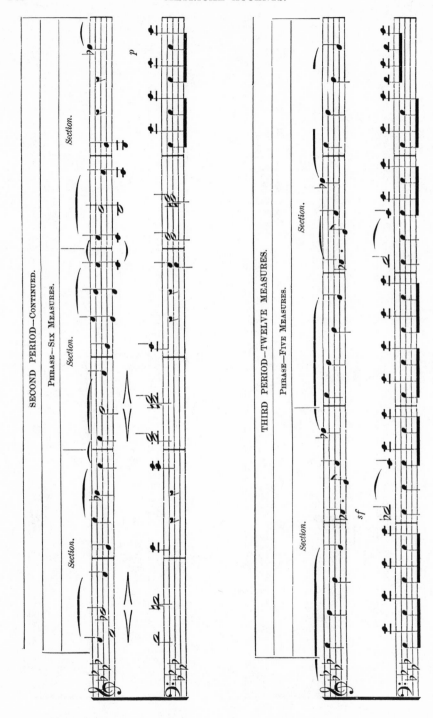

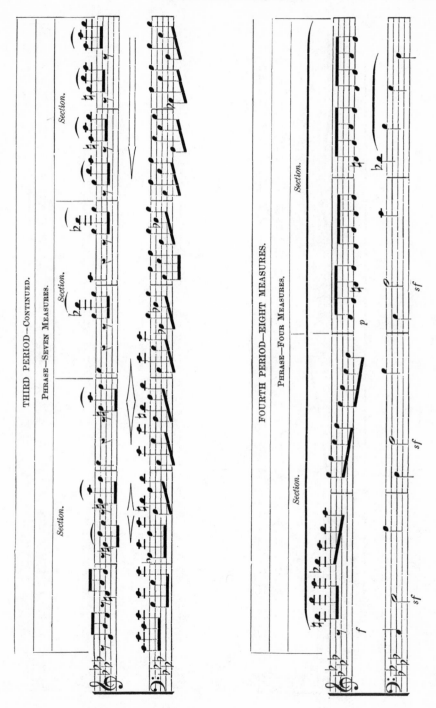

THIRD PERIOD—Continued.

Phrase—Seven Measures.

FOURTH PERIOD—EIGHT MEASURES.

Phrase—Four Measures.

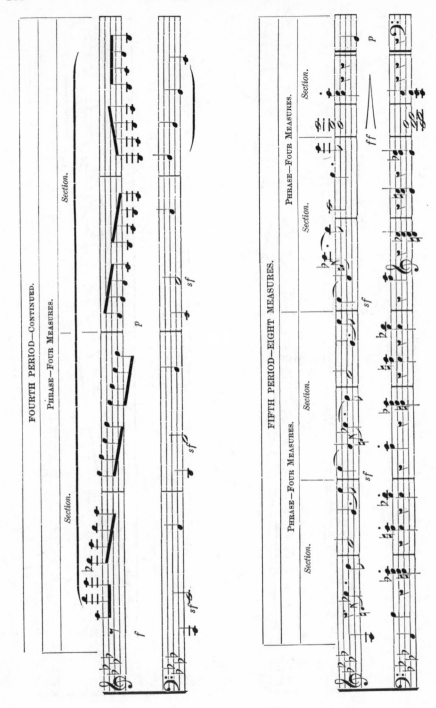

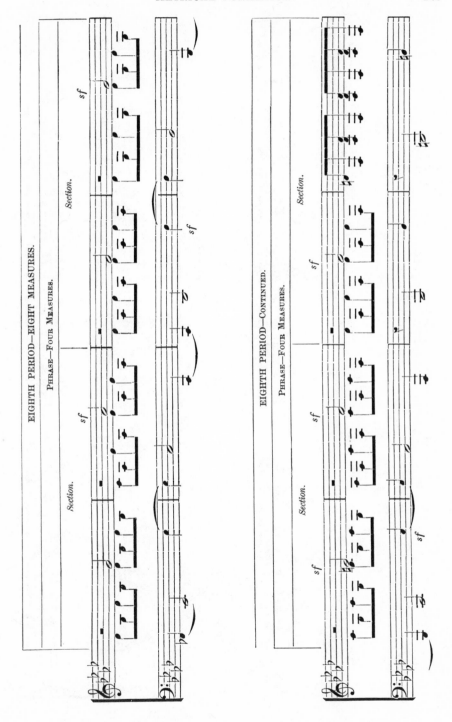

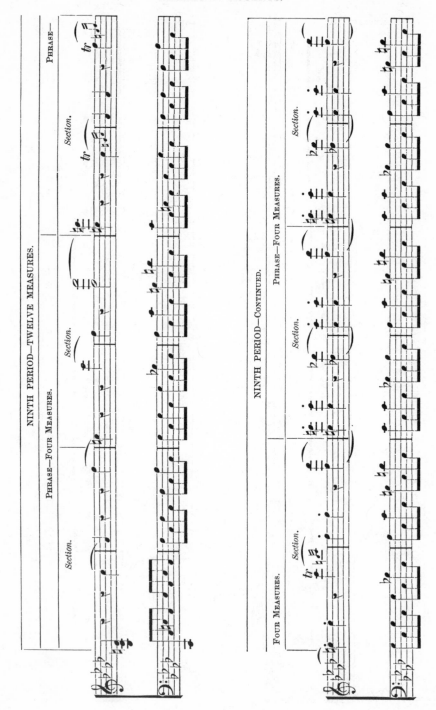

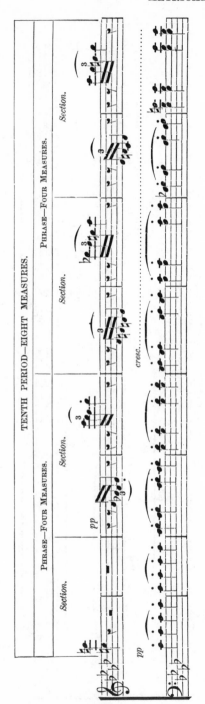

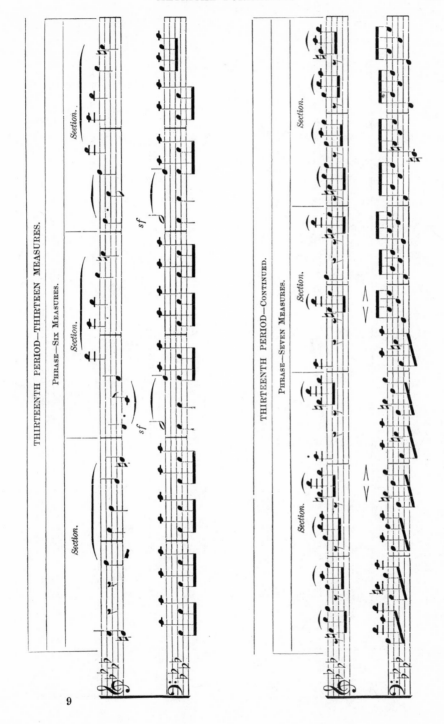

THIRTEENTH PERIOD—THIRTEEN MEASURES.

PHRASE—SIX MEASURES.

THIRTEENTH PERIOD—Continued.

PHRASE—SEVEN MEASURES.

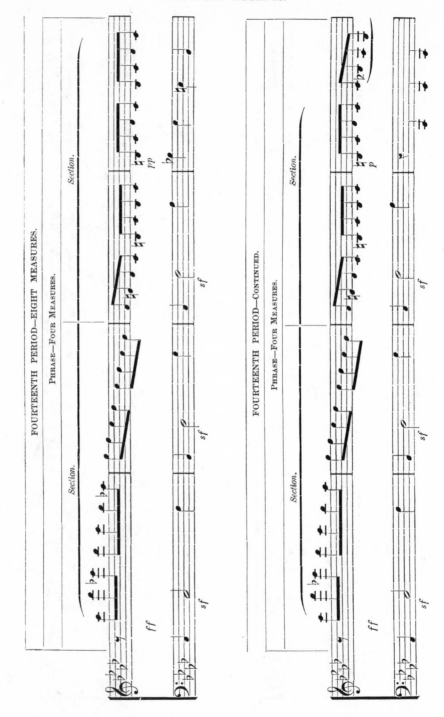

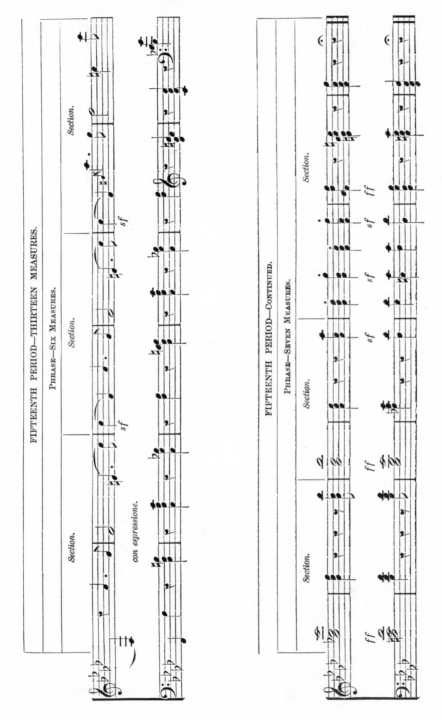

None of these periods and phrases present any new feature for remark. The entire movement has been given in order to exemplify the mode of proceeding in periodizing (in a like manner) other compositions.

In view of aiding the student still more in becoming familiar with this metrical work, I subjoin a few additional examples.

BEETHOVEN—SONATA, Op. 2, No. 1.

MENUETTO.	TRIO.
First Period—14 Measures.	*Fourth Period*—10 Measures.
3 Phrases of 4 : 4 : 6 Measures.	2 Phrases of 4 : 6 Measures.
7 Sections of 2 2 : 2 2 : 2 2 2 "	5 Sections of 2 2 : 2 2 2 "
Second Period—14 Measures.	*Fifth Period*—15 Measures.
3 Phrases of 4 : 6 : 4 Measures.	2 Phrases of 7 : 8 Measures.
7 Sections of 2 2 : 2 2 2 : 2 2 "	6 Sections of 2 2 3 : 2 3 3 "
Third Period—12 Measures.	*Sixth Period*—8 Measures.
2 Phrases of 6 : 6 Measures.	2 Phrases of 4 : 4 Measures.
6 Sections of 2 2 2 : 2 2 2 "	4 Sections of 2 2 : 2 2 "

Menuetto da Capo.

BEETHOVEN—SONATA, Op. 26.

ANDANTE CON VARIAZIONI.	*Fifth Period*—12 Measures.
First and Second Periods—Regular.	3 Phrases of 4 : 4 : 4 Measures.
	6 Sections of 2 2 : 2 2 : 2 2 "
Third Period—10 Measures.	
2 Phrases of 4 : 6 Measures.	*Sixth Period*—Regular.
5 Sections of 2 2 : 2 2 2 "	
	Seventh Period—15 Measures.
Fourth Period—Regular.	3 Phrases of 4 : 4 : 7 Measures.
The five Variations contain the same Pe-	7 Sections of 2 2 : 2 2 : 2 2 3 "
riods.	
The fifth Variation has the following Coda:	TRIO.
Coda Period—15 Measures.	*Eighth, Ninth and Tenth Periods*—Regular
3 Phrases of 4 : 4 : 7 Measures.	*Tenth Period* (second time)—12 Measures.
7 Sections of 2 2 : 2 2 : 2 2 3 "	
	3 Phrases of 4 : 4 : 4 Measures.
SCHERZO.	6 Sections of 2 2 : 2 2 : 2 2 "
First, Second, Third and Fourth Periods—	
Regular.	*Scherzo da Capo.*

MARCIA FUNÈBRE.

First Period—Regular.

Second Period—12 Measures.

3 Phrases of 4   : 4   : 4   Measures.
6 Sections of 2 2 : 2 2 : 2 2   "

Third Period—10 Measures.

2 Phrases of 4   : 6   Measures.
5 Sections of 2 2 : 2 2 2   "

‖: *Fourth Period*—Regular, including repetition. :‖

‖: *Fifth Period*—Regular, including repetition. :‖

Sixth Period—Regular.

Seventh Period—12 Measures.

3 Phrases of 4   : 4   : 4   Measures.
6 Sections of 2 2 : 2 2 : 2 2   "

Eighth Period—17 Measures.

3 Phrases of 4   : 6   : 7   Measures.
8 Sections of 2 2 : 2 2 2 : 2 2 3   "

Although I have limited the extent of irregular periods, as a rule, to fifteen measures, this does not, by any means, exclude an occasional period of more than fifteen measures, as exemplified in the Marcia Funèbre.

The two last periods in the march (containing together twenty-nine measures) might have been arranged in three periods of eight, eight, and thirteen measures respectively, in order to avoid the long period of seventeen measures.

But there was no need of such avoidance, and, moreover, such division would have cut into the unity of the seventh period which, being identical with the second period, required twelve measures, not eight. Therefore the unity of the seventh period had to be repeated.

This left us seventeen measures, which might have been divided into two periods of eight and nine measures respectively. But here again, considerations of unity decided that these seventeen measures contained three phrases of four, six, and seven measures respectively, hence were one period, not two periods.

Although rare, this is not an isolated case of a seventeen-measured period, in evidence of which I here give another one.

SCHUMANN—In der Nacht, Op. 12, No. 5.

PERIOD—SEVENTEEN MEASURES.

First Phrase—Seven Measures.

Section—Three Measures.

First Phrase—Continued.

Section—Two Measures.

Section—Two Measures.

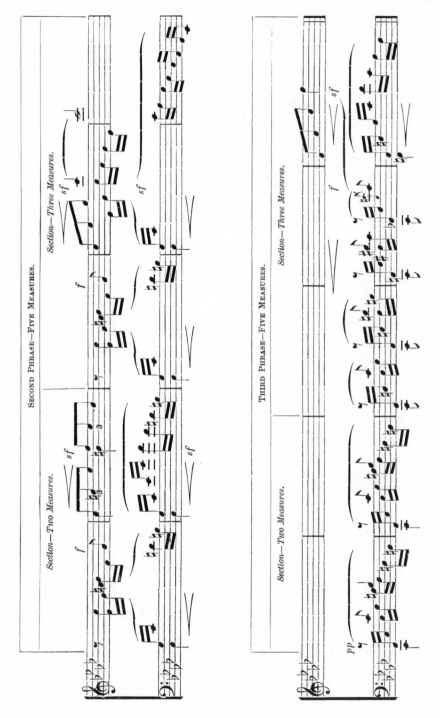

The above period leaves not the slightest doubt as to its unity. It is terminated by a double bar $\left(\mathbb{E} \right)$, Schumann's own indication, and is also shown by the reappearance of the first subject in the eighteenth or next measure.

Its phrases also are distinctly defined by the reappearance of the first subject, after the termination of each phrase; and, by reason of this phrasing alone, the period could not be cut into two periods.

The sections, likewise, leave no doubt as to their unity. As a last example, I shall periodize the remainder of:

SCHUMANN—In der Nacht, Op. 12, No. 5.

Second Period—9 Measures.

2 Phrases of 4   : 5   Measures.
5 Sections of 2 2 : 2 3   "

Third Period—Regular.

Fourth Period—10 Measures.

2 Phrases of 5   : 5   Measures.
4 Sections of 2 3 : 2 3   "

Fifth Period—12 Measures.

2 Phrases of 7   : 5   Measures.
5 Sections of 3 2 2 : 2 3   "

Sixth Period—12 Measures.

2 Phrases of 5   : 7   Measures.
5 Sections of 2 3 : 2 2·3   "

———

Etwas langsamer.

Seventh Period—Regular.

Eighth Period—Regular.

Ninth Period—Regular.

Tenth Period—Regular.

Eleventh Period—Regular.

Twelfth Period—13 Measures.

3 Phrases of 4   : 5   : 4   Measures.
6 Sections of 2 2 : 2 3 : 2 2   "

Thirteenth Period—Regular.

Fourteenth Period—14 Measures.

3 Phrases of 4   : 4   : 6   Measures.
7 Sections of 2 2 : 2 2 : 2 2 2   "

Fifteenth Period—17 Measures (from beginning).

3 Phrases of 7   : 5   : 5   Measures.
7 Sections of 3 2 2 : 2 3 : 2 3   "

Sixteenth Period—11 Measures.

2 Phrases of 6   : 5   Measûres.
5 Sections of 2 2 : 2 3   "

Seventeenth Period—Regular.

Eighteenth Period—10 Measures.

2 Phrases of 5   : 5   Measures.
4 Sections of 2 3 : 2 3   "

Nineteenth Period—12 Measures.

2 Phrases of 5   : 7   Measures.
5 Sections of 3 2 : 2 2 3   "

Twentieth Period—12 Measures.

3 Phrases of 4   : 4   : 4   Measures.
6 Sections of 2 2 : 2 2 : 2 2   "

Twenty-first Period—10 Measures.

2 Phrases of 4   : 6   Measures.
5 Sections of 2 2 : 2 2 2   "

The examples of periods, phrases, and sections, so far given, have shown us these metrical groups in almost every combination in which they may be actually met with.

We have had Sections of 2 and 3 Measures,
Phrases of 4, 5, 6, and 7 Measures, and
Periods of 8, 9, 10, 11, 12, 13, 14, 15, and 17 Measures,

—a sufficiently exhaustive variety of combinations, to cover and explain every case of metrical analysis.

No composition can be really understood, unless the mind is able to define its periods, phrases, and sections.

Discrimination of these metrical groups becomes a revelation, and periodizing is the source of this revelation.

Many an uninteresting, because not comprehended, composition becomes of surprising interest, when the finer thoughts of the composer's *architectonic* are brought to light.

As the reader's mind discerns these *architectonic* phrases, so should he, as interpreter, convey them to his audience through the means of metrical accentuation, at the beginning and at the proper breaks between the groups.

Metrical accentuation is only difficult intellectually, not mechanically ; for, as soon as the student is thoroughly efficient in periodizing, he will then also know when and where to accent metrically.

PART III.

MELODIC ACCENTS.

GENERAL OBSERVATIONS.

MELODY is a pleasing succession of musical sounds rhythmically arranged. The character of melody depends mainly on its rhythmical arrangement and the tempo, as by the change of either rhythm or tempo (or both) the character may be so altered as to produce a different effect.

Many a lively opera melody has thus been turned into sacred music, and the most solemn airs travestied into dance-tunes.

Melody is the golden thread running through the maze of tones, by which the ear is guided and the heart reached. Without melody, music may interest, but cannot charm ; fortunately, music without melody is not conceivable. The simplest and most monotonous kind of music has melody, although its character may not be to the liking of every one. The noisiest and most complicated music has melody ; but it may be so laden with external flourishes, or so obscured by internal changes, that few only can detect and follow the golden thread. Or there may be more than one thread, as in polyphonous music ; two, three, or four melodies, so intermingled that it becomes an effort, instead of being a pleasure, to follow any of them. Then again, the thread may be disjointed and cut into little bits, as in thematic work, where a subject is so twisted, imitated and turned around, that most people perceive neither head nor tail of the melody.

Thematic work is the artistic manipulation of a short musical subject ; an almost infinite variety of transformations, repetitions, additions, imitations, etc., by means of which the smallest subject is developed into a work of art.

Thematic work is the outcome of contrapuntal study. Both contrapuntal writing and thematic work have their climax in the fugue. The fugue, however, although being the highest scientific form, is not the highest artistic form, but simply an accessory to the latter.

The highest artistic form, in pianoforte music, is the sonata; in orchestral music, the symphony.

It seems strange, but it is, nevertheless, true, that the public cares no longer for fugues and very little for sonatas. Very few artists attempt to write either, and yet every one acknowledges Bach's fugues and Beethoven's sonatas as the unapproachable patterns of these respective classical forms, while Von Bülow very wittily and appropriately calls the former "the old testament of pianoforte literature," and the latter, "the new testament."

Artistically, melody is of the least account, for any one, with very little talent, can compose a melody; and it is natural, that the more trivial or silly the melody is, the more it approaches the taste and understanding of the multitude.

But not every one can compose a good melody, or harmonize it properly, still less, work it out into artistic form.

By far the greater number of modern pianoforte compositions are not artistic, and are written in the simplest of all forms—that of dances, marches, or songs; viz.:

Four parts (sometimes six or eight), with an introduction at the beginning, and a tail at the end. After this pattern:

INTRODUCTION ; First Part, Second Part, Third Part.
TRIO ; Third Part, Fourth Part, Third Part.
First and Second Part.
CODA—(*Fine.*)

This kind of musical form every one understands; each part being a complete melody of eight or sixteen measures, each melody a separate part. When one melody or part is finished, another begins, as in a panorama— here is one picture, here is another.

The general public expects something like the above form in all compositions; plain, fully developed melodies succeeding each other. Hence, it is not surprising that the effect of a really artistic or classical work should be rather bewildering than enjoyable; and I can quite understand how an unmusical, though clever, Frenchwoman, while listening to the performance of one of Beethoven's sonatas, should remark to her neighbor: "Dites donc, ami, l'introduction est bien longue."

The first educational step towards becoming an intelligent listener, is the appreciation of variations. This trains the ear to recognize a theme through all its external disguises, or internal transformations, and leads to the comprehension of thematic work, which is indispensable for judging and enjoying classical music.

A theme is understood to mean the leading melody, but need not necessarily be a fully developed melody ; for it may be long or short, as in fugues, and sometimes a simple subject merely.

But, whether a theme be long or short, its thematic treatment is mostly restricted to a part of the theme only, generally its elementary subject (or motive).

A subject being more easily handled than a whole theme, has always played a greater rôle in the art of composing than the theme itself ; and it seems destined to be of still greater importance in the music of the future.

To the prophets of this future school a short subject is of paramount importance, a fully developed theme of secondary moment. Wagner, particularly, is very liberal with his subjects—little snatches of short, unfinished thoughts—introducing many, but developing few. His subjects are generally in a state of fermentation, but rarely becoming a good, honest melody ; and when the latter now and then appears, it seems to be merely a concession to the public.

In orchestral music, the repetitions and imitations of a subject are more plainly discerned, and more interesting, than in pianoforte music, on account of the coloring of the different instruments. In pianoforte music, this coloring has to be supplied by accentuation.

Here we come to the first class of melodic accents.

CHAPTER V.

THEMATIC ACCENTS.

MUSIC, with only one melody—whether accompanied or not, whether one person is the performer or a thousand persons—is said to be *homophonous, i. e.*, one-voiced.

Music, with more than one melody—two, three, four, or more voices appearing simultaneously or successively, each voice having its own melody, going its own way—is said to be *polyphonous, i. e.*, many-voiced.

All contrapuntal music is polyphonous, its very name implying a counter-point, or counter-melody.

Classical music is generally polyphonous.

Modern music is mostly homophonous.

Now, with regard to thematic accents, I would call attention to the difference of "accenting a theme" and "giving prominence to it."

As a matter of course, a theme should stand out prominently from its accompaniment and the arabesques that may be woven around it. This needed conspicuousness of the theme is not, however, a question of accentuation, but one of *dynamics;* because, when a whole row of notes (as in a melody) is played louder than another row (the accompaniment), this cannot be called accenting, for accenting refers to individual points.

Therefore, to accent a theme does not mean to accent every note of it, but *to emphasize the beginning of the theme only.*

The emphasis on the beginning is necessary, in order to call attention to the theme's appearance, or reappearance, after a temporary rest.

When polyphonous music has an accompaniment, the voices carrying the melodies should have the same prominence over the accompaniment that the single melody has in homophonous music. But the different voices, being of equal importance, should be of equal quality, and blend harmoniously together. Greater power of one voice would impair the blending, and assert for itself a prominence which none should have, unless it were a solo voice.

A solo voice in polyphonous music, a *cantus firmus* in counter-point, or the melody in homophonous music, *need not be accented thematically;* *i. e.*, the initial note need not be emphasized, because the quality of tone in all such cases is supposed to be already sufficiently prominent to assert itself above the surroundings, without any special emphasis on the opening note.

Through this simple rule we dispense at once with the greater number of cases in which thematic accents might seem to be applicable, and we reduce their application to polyphonous music alone, viz.: where there are more than one melodic voice.

Having so far discussed the negative side of thematic accents, *i. e.*, where they are not to be given, I now come to the other side—where they are to be given.

In all polyphonous music, each voice or theme requires an emphasis on the first or opening note, for the purpose of denoting the theme's entrance.

This rule is so simple, that it needs little explanation; none being necessary with regard to strict contrapuntal forms, such as fugues, canons, etc. But I shall give a few examples from modern music, showing the application of thematic accents, when different voices freely imitate a theme.

SCHUMANN—Nachtstück, Op. 23, No. 4.

The accents and slurs in this example are mine. These may explain the phrasing and thematic accents which Schumann thought it unnecessary to indicate.

It is also of importance to observe that the tone of the theme-giving and responding voices should be of equal quality, but superior in power to that of the accompanying notes. This is an imperative condition which must be complied with, though its execution requires considerable independence and discrimination of touch.

SCHUMANN—Warum? Op. 12, No. 3.

Syncopic Accent.

This example is similar to the former.

Both are two-voiced (*zwei-stimmig*); the rest, accompaniment.

The imitations are free; *i. e.,* the intervals of the responses are not strictly the same as in the theme-giving voice. For example:

this being the theme,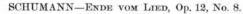

and this the response,

it will be seen, at a glance, that the steps of the latter are not the same as those of the former.

I have altered the slurs, in order to indicate the unity of the responses, so as to make them correspond with the unity of the theme.

SCHUMANN—ENDE VOM LIED, Op. 12, No. 8.

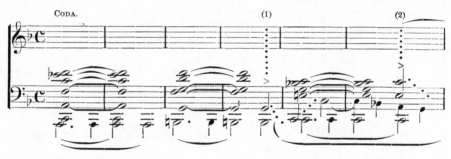

(1) Entrance of part of theme.   (2) Entrance of first theme (enlarged).

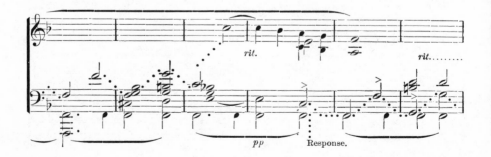

Response.

The original theme of this example has been enlarged in the Coda, by doubling the value of each note.

Coda.

Such enlargement is one of the many modes of transformation.

Mention has been made of an external and internal treatment of a theme.

Let us explain.

A theme may remain intact, though surrounded by *external* figuring. In strict form, such an unaltered theme is called *cantus firmus;* and the surrounding figuring, the counterpoint or counterpoints. In free form, it is simply *the melody;* and the flourishing around, the variations (as in the style of Thalberg).

10

Or, a theme may be transformed *internally* by thematic work. in a multitude of ways.

As it is desirable that the student should be conversant with these several modes, in order to recognize a theme readily, notwithstanding its internal changes or transformations, I here give an enumeration of these modes.

THEMATIC TRANSFORMATION.

Taking the first phrase of Schumann's "Warum?" as our theme,

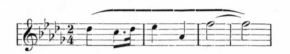

we shall see what thematic work can do with it.

1. Simple Modes of Tonic Transformation.

1. The theme may be removed (versetzt); *i. e.*, the opening note may be removed to any other interval, the steps of each note remaining the same.

2. It may be contracted (verengert); *i. e.*, the steps of each interval may be contracted.

3. It may be extended (erweitert), viz.: in the steps of its intervals.

4. Or inverted (verkehrt).

2. Simple Modes of Rhythmical Transformation.

5. The theme may be enlarged (vergrössert), viz.: each interval.

6. Or diminished (verkleinert).

7. Or curtailed (verkürzt).

8. Or lengthened, by repeating the curtailed theme.

9. Or lengthened, by adding new links to the curtailed theme.

10. Or transformed, by varying the whole theme; (this is internal variation.)

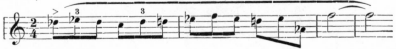

3. Combined Modes of Tonic and Rhythmic Transformation. Two Modes Combined.

11. The theme may be removed and contracted—1 and 2.

12. It may be removed and extended—1 and 3.

13. It may be removed and inverted—1 and 4.

14. It may be contracted and inverted—2 and 4.

15. It may be removed and enlarged—1 and 5.

16. It may be removed and diminished—1 and 6.

17. It may be enlarged and inverted—5 and 4.

18. It may be diminished and inverted—6 and 4.

19. It may be removed and varied—1 and 10.

20. It may be removed and curtailed—1 and 7.

21. It may be removed and lengthened—1 and 8.

22. It may be removed and added to—1 and 9.

23. It may be contracted and enlarged—2 and 5.

24. It may be contracted and diminished—2 and 6.

25. It may be contracted and curtailed—2 and 7.

26. It may be contracted and lengthened—2 and 3.

27. It may be extended and added to—2 and 9.

28. It may be extended and inverted—3 and 4.

29. It may be extended and enlarged—3 and 5.

30. It may be extended and diminished—3 and 6.

31. It may be extended and curtailed—3 and 7.

To save space, I give the rest of this enumeration without illustrations.

32. A theme may be extended and lengthened—3 and 8.
33. A theme may be extended and added to—3 and 9.
34. A theme may be inverted and curtailed—4 and 7.
35. A theme may be inverted and lengthened—4 and 8.
36. A theme may be inverted and added to—4 and 9.
37. A theme may be enlarged and curtailed—5 and 7.
38. A theme may be enlarged and lengthened—5 and 8.
39. A theme may be enlarged and added to—5 and 9.
40. A theme may be diminished and curtailed—6 and 7.
41. A theme may be diminished and lengthened—6 and 8.
42. A theme may be diminished and added to—6 and 9.
43. A theme may be curtailed and lengthened—7 and 8.
44. A theme may be curtailed and added to—7 and 9.
45. A theme may be lengthened and added to—8 and 9.

4. Three Combined Modes.

46. A theme may be removed, contracted, and inverted—1 2 4.
47. A theme may be removed, extended, and inverted—1 3 4.
48. A theme may be removed, enlarged, and inverted—1 5 4.
49. A theme may be removed, diminished, and inverted—1 6 4.
50. A theme may be removed, inverted, and curtailed—1 4 7.
51. A theme may be removed, inverted, and lengthened—1 4 8.
52. A theme may be removed, inverted, and added to—1 4 9.
53. A theme may be contracted, inverted, and enlarged—2 4 5.
54. A theme may be contracted, inverted, and diminished—2 4 6.
55. A theme may be contracted, inverted, and curtailed—2 4 7.
56. A theme may be contracted, inverted, and lengthened—2 4 8.
57. A theme may be contracted, inverted, and added to—2 4 9.
58. A theme may be extended, inverted, and enlarged—3 4 5.
59. A theme may be extended, inverted, and diminished—3 4 6.
60. A theme may be extended, inverted, and curtailed—3 4 7.
61. A theme may be extended, inverted, and lengthened—3 4 8.
62. A theme may be extended, inverted, and added to—3 4 9.
63. A theme may be enlarged, curtailed, and lengthened—5 7 8.
64. A theme may be enlarged, curtailed, and added to—5 7 9.
65. A theme may be diminished, curtailed, and lengthened—6 7 8.
66. A theme may be diminished, curtailed, and added to—6 7 9.
67. A theme may be curtailed, lengthened, and added to—7 8 9.

5. Four Combined Modes.

68. A theme may be removed, contracted, inverted, and enlarged—
1 2 4 5.

69. A theme may be removed, contracted, inverted, and diminished—
1 2 4 6.

70. A theme may be removed, contracted, inverted, and curtailed—
1 2 4 7.

71. A theme may be removed, contracted, inverted, and lengthened—
1 2 4 8.

72. A theme may be removed, extended, inverted, and enlarged—
1 3 4 5.

73. A theme may be removed, extended, inverted, and diminished—
1 3 4 6.

74. A theme may be removed, extended, inverted, and curtailed— 1 3 4 7.

75. A theme may be removed, extended, inverted, and lengthened— 1 3 4 8.

76. A theme may be contracted, inverted, enlarged, and curtailed— 2 4 5 7.

77. A theme may be contracted, inverted, enlarged, and lengthened— 2 4 5 8.

78. A theme may be contracted, inverted, enlarged, and added to— 2 4 5 9.

79. A theme may be contracted, inverted, diminished, and curtailed— 2 4 6 7.

80. A theme may be contracted, inverted, diminished, and lengthened— 2 4 6 8.

81. A theme may be contracted, inverted, diminished, and added to— 2 4 6 9.

82. A theme may be contracted, inverted, curtailed, and lengthened— 2 4 7 8.

83. A theme may be contracted, inverted, lengthened, and added to— 2 4 8 9.

84. A theme may be enlarged, curtailed, lengthened, and added to— 5 7 8 9.

85. A theme may be diminished, curtailed, lengthened, and added to— 6 7 8 9.

5. Five Combined Modes of Transformation.

86. It may be removed, contracted, inverted, enlarged, and lengthened—1 2 4 5 8.

87. It may be removed, contracted, inverted, enlarged, and added to 1 2 4 5 9.

And so on.

I take this enumeration from Lobe's "Compositions-Lehre" (Weimar; 1844), giving it without alteration or addition, excepting the illustration.

Although this is, by no means, an exhaustive enumeration, it conveys a fair idea of the extent and capabilities of thematic work, and is more than sufficient for the present purpose.

Most of these modes are classed and taught under " *Imitations*," these being part of contrapuntal study, preceding fugues and canons.

Imitations are either strict or free.

When both the value and the steps of each note are precisely imitated, it is called strict imitation; otherwise, it is free imitation.

The former is naturally restricted, while the latter is almost boundless, reaching to an extent where the imitation leaves hardly a trace of the original theme, and the transformation ceases almost to be an imitation.

To all those interested in, and desirous of, becoming familiar with thematic work, I recommend Lobe's excellent treatise, which deserves to, and probably would, be more generally known, were it not overshadowed by the author's later and greater work, entitled also " Compositions-Lehre," published in four volumes, at Leipzig.

CHAPTER VI.

ACCENTS OF EXTREMES.

MUSIC, more particularly, melody, being a succession of ascending and descending sounds, must now and then in its motion reach some extreme high or low point, on which it is natural that the voice should lay an especial stress.

This stress—here called accent of extremes—is generally the culminating point of a *crescendo*.

By a natural law, the stress of the voice increases when ascending, and decreases when descending; yet this rule has its exceptions as well as any other rule. The very opposite may be necessary. Descending notes may require a *crescendo*, and ascending ones a *diminuendo;* therefore, the lower extreme has also a right to emphasis.

It seems hardly necessary to explain " extremes," yet I will illustrate them symbolically, thus:

In this zig-zag motion, the turning-points are not all accented, at least not so perceptibly as to deserve the name of accent; because—a melodic accent being like a knot in the thread of melody which is tied for the purpose of calling attention to it—too many knots, or accents, would rather mar than improve the thread of melody.

When a *crescendo* has reached the culminating point, which it is necessary to mark by special emphasis, it is desirable also, and quite natural, that this extreme point should be slightly dwelt upon, in addition to the given emphasis.

This imparts to the accented point a more pronounced emphasis than it is possible to give without it.

But dwelling on the accented extreme must not be exaggerated; for example:

WEBER—Concertstück, Op. 79.

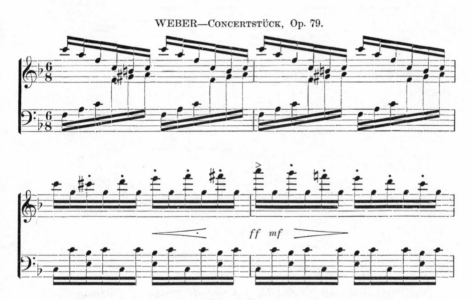

Another means of increasing the effect of extreme accents is that of letting the emphatic force, which falls on the extreme point, be succeeded by *suddenly* diminished strength, instead of by a general *diminuendo;* for example:

MENDELSSOHN—Concerto, Op. 25 (G-Minor).

Observe now the motion of the two last examples:

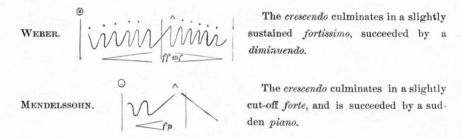

WEBER. The *crescendo* culminates in a slightly sustained *fortissimo*, succeeded by a *diminuendo*.

MENDELSSOHN. The *crescendo* culminates in a slightly cut-off *forte*, and is succeeded by a sudden *piano*.

When, in giving an extreme accent, these means are combined, viz.: when

1st. The culminating point of a *crescendo* is strongly accented;

2d. A slight dwelling on the accented note is added;

3d. And the emphatic force of the accented point is succeeded by suddenly diminished strength;

then, the effect is of the most pronounced kind, even if the performer has only very little strength at his disposal.

For it is never so much the banging and pounding of undisciplined crude force, which produces such good effects, as the judicious and calculating grading of strength, the holding back, until the right moment arrives.

The dwelling upon, or rather, prolongation of a note is a necessity to an extreme accent; without it, the impression would be that of a passing *crescendo*, instead of an accented point.

It is not, however, so much the dwelling upon a note, or the sustaining of it, which is needed, as the prolongation of the accented point. There is considerable distinction in this.

For, instead of sustaining the accented extreme note, the latter is frequently cut short, like a sharp smack, and then prolonged by a waiting, viz., the note is cut short, the time on the extreme point is prolonged. This necessitates a slight *accelerando* and shortening of some of the succeeding notes, in order to make up for loss of time. See, for example, the following from Mendelssohn:

Composer's Notation.   Altered Notation.

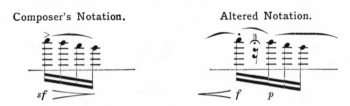

According to the alteration, the first note of the group belongs to the preceding slur and is a terminating extreme, instead of a commencing one, as in Mendelssohn's notation.

Although such alteration is occasionally of good effect, as in the above example, yet it is always a liberty taken with the composition, which should only sparingly be resorted to.

The accessory means of marking extreme points, by shortening and prolonging them, may be quite justifiable occasionally, but must not be abused, as it so frequently is.

About the time when Schulhoff's once favorite, "Souvenir de Varsovie," appeared (twenty-five years ago), it was quite the fashion to throw off, so to say, the extreme point of ascending runs, and then pause a moment. But, like most fashions, this method became exaggerated to such an extent, that it reached the height of affectation, and, fortunately, was checked by an awakening better taste.

No nation abused this way of shortening little runs, and pausing after it, so much as the French; and no composer's works suffered by it so much as Chopin's; for example:

CHOPIN—VALSE, Op. posthumous, No. 4 (Op. 69, No. 1).

This little waltz has three ascending runs of a similar character:

These runs illustrate admirably the excessive affectation, with which the pianoforte-playing public used to spoil such passages, through prolonging beyond measure the little rest, 𝄽, after the extreme note. (I cite this example, in memory of personal afflictions of this sort during a residence in France.)

Excessive waiting, after a shortened point, is always bad; while the little pause, when given in moderation, has a beautiful effect.

The shortening of an extreme note may be quite necessary, even when not indicated, or when the contrary is indicated; for example:

CHOPIN—VALSE, Op. 64, No. 1.

The shortening of the extreme B-flat (which is not Chopin's notation) gives a finish, a certain *cachet* to the ascending passage, which seems to me so natural and indispensable, that I cannot believe Chopin could have intended it to be otherwise.

His own slurring,  , cannot be correct,

because the B-flat evidently terminates the run, and could not be preceded by a break on the G-flat, as Chopin's notation calls for. Hence, the B-flat should be included in the slur.

It is another thing, however, with the second B-flat, two measures further on. There, the slur, instead of ending, commences a phrase, and the B-flat is not shortened.

Another contrast would be that of playing this little ascending run, the second time, *diminuendo*.

The shortening of an extreme note is also effectively employed as a means of giving new force and pith to extreme points, when similar groups or passages are repeated; for example:

CHOPIN—VALSE, Op. 34.

First time.   *Second time.*

As a rule, *any group or figure, when repeated, should be rendered in a different way, to avoid sameness.*

This is especially necessary when any little phrase or figure occurs three or more times in succession. (See, for example, Chopin's Fourth Prelude, which, simple as it appears, requires very serious study with respect to discrimination of strength.)

One repetition unchanged, might pass; but two repetitions without a change become monotonous, and necessitate alteration.

Such alteration may be an augmentation or diminution of emphasis, a lengthening or shortening of the extremes, etc.

In the majority of cases, it is that of increasing intensity toward the last repetition, such as : *piano, mezzoforte, forte.*

But the alteration may be made in many other ways, as the occasion demands, and without following any stereotyped rule.

So far I have considered these accents of extremes as referring solely to the highest and lowest notes of runs and passages; their range, however, is a much more extended one, for one may almost include in them the next class of melodic accents.

CHAPTER VII.

ACCENTS OF SLURS.

HERE, likewise, the extremes are accented. Not, however, the highest and lowest notes; but the first and last, or the opening and finishing notes, in any slurred group.

Although a slur, in its general meaning, is simply a *legato* indication, yet (in lack of a more appropriate collective sign) it has also the special function of grouping together a number of notes into a unity, which we call *a phrase*.

The accentuation of a slurred phrase may be exemplified by the throwing of a stone:

☞ Motion.

The opening and finishing notes, or the two extremes of the slur, are the strong and accented points.

The opening extreme has the energy of throwing; the terminal note, that of contact; and the *legato* motion within should be as smooth and even as the flight of the stone.

The accents on the opening and finishing points envelop the motion and define the limit of the slur, by denoting the limit audibly.

The two extreme points, however, are not of equal force.

The opening point is strong, when falling on a strong time-part:

And weak, when falling on a weak time-part:

In a like manner, the endings are either strong or weak, in accordance with the time-parts they fall on.

FIRST RULE.

a. *Strong beginnings and endings of slurred groups are always accented.*

This is explicit enough.

b. *Weak beginnings of slurred groups are accented only when commencing a leading subject, and descending.*

This I exemplify by the following illustrations :

WEBER—Rondeau of Sonata, Op. 24, in C-Major

WEBER—Rondeau Brillant, Op. 62.

c. *Weak endings are never accented.*

The opening note of a slur, when accented, has the weight of touch, drawing after it, so to say, the succeeding notes ; of course, decreasingly,

The mechanical operation is this : The touch comes down on the keys from the arm, with or without the aid of the wrist ; and, while the fingers alone are playing (without pressure), the arm follows the direction of the fingers.

When the initial note is not accented, the touch begins gently and increases toward the culminating point of the slur, which is either in the centre, or at the end of the slur, viz. :

either so, ⟨image⟩, or so, ⟨image⟩.

11

But the most important thing to be observed in a slurred phrase— more important even than the accent denoting its beginning—is the short- ening of the final note, in order to denote the termination of the phrase.

SECOND RULE.

The final note of slurred groups, whether accented or not, should be shortened to about one-half of its noted value.

This rule has few exceptions.

To terminate a phrase comprehensively, it is absolutely necessary to shorten the final note.

If the final note were not shortened, but sustained, this sustaining would prevent or suspend the termination, and necessitate a drawing-over to the next note, or still further, until a rest were reached, where the finger could be raised and a cessation of sound effected. Hence, the final note is only then really terminal, when followed by a rest. And it follows, that a slur (as phrase-indication) should not terminate with a note that is to be sustained, but should end either before or after a sustained note.

For example, this slurring, ♪♪♪♪ | ♩, is faulty; for it does not effect a perfect termination, and, to be correct, should be either so, ♪♪♪♪ | ♩, or so, ♪♪♪♪ | ♩ ♩, or so, ♪♪♪♪ | ♩ · ♪, etc.

A considerable part of musical interpunction depends on a due observ- ance of this rule, and if composers were to follow it, their slurring would be more exact and rational than it now is.

If it be irrational to terminate a slur with a sustained note, or a note prolonged beyond its value, it is also irrational to terminate the slur with a long note, viz.: a longer one than that preceding the final note.

THIRD RULE.

It is a natural, though unwritten law, that *the terminating note of a slurred group shall be shorter than the preceding one, or, at least, shall not surpass it in length.*

Starting from this rule, the slur is best terminated when the final note is the shortest of the group; whereas the termination becomes less and less definite, less precise, less satisfactory in proportion as the final note in- creases in duration.

Compare, for example, the following slur-terminations:

1. This is best:

2. This is good:

3. This is allowable:

4. This is doubtful: and

5. This is bad : ⎫
               ⎬ Here the excep-
                 tions come in.
6. This is worse :⎭

Nos. 1 and 2 of these terminations do not require explanation.

No. 3 is "allowable," because, the final note being shortened to one-half of its noted value, it becomes thus reduced to equal the value of the preceding note.

No. 4.   This slurring is only doubtfully correct as a phrase-indication, but may pass as a *legato*-indication, especially when in practice the final note is shortened a little more than half its value.

Beethoven, who may be taken as a pattern of correct slurring, generally avoids it, though he employs it occasionally, when he cannot otherwise indicate a *legato*.   For example ·

SONATA, Op. 14.   SONATA PATHETIQUE.

Nos. 5 and 6.   But, when the final note is of such disproportionate length as here (eight or sixteen times as long as the preceding note), the slurring is either

a. Wrong, because not being far enough extended, or too far extended.

b. Or it is incorrect, because belonging to the few exceptions where it can be logically accounted for.

These exceptions will be discussed further on.   For the present, I shall exemplify a few cases where the composer's slurring is incorrect.

I. The Slurring not being far enough Extended.

MENDELSSOHN—Capriccio Brillante, Op. 22.

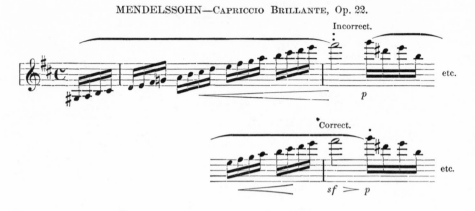

WEBER—Invitation to the Dance.

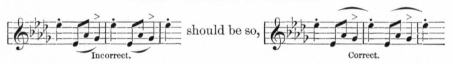

should be so,

A slur may also be extended to a rest; for example:

CHOPIN—Ballade, Op. 23.

Would not this slurring be more correct?—

It is certainly quite logical, and suggests itself naturally to the intelligent performer.

2. The Slurring being too far Extended.

The following illustrations are from Klindworth's edition of Chopin.

MARCHE FUNÈBRE, Op. 35.

The Slurring, as written :

As it ought to be :

NOCTURNE, Op. 9, No. 2.

As written :

As it ought to be :

NOCTURNE, Op. 9, No. 2.

As written :

As it ought to be :

NOCTURNE, Op. 9, No. 2.

As written :   *As it ought to be :*

SONATA, Op. 58.

These are only small instances, but such may be counted by the thousand, and are to be met with in almost all pianoforte works.

Schumann is very careful in his slurring; Chopin is less so. Only Beethoven is here, as in other cases, a rare example of correctness.

Glancing through Beethoven's sonatas (latest Breitkopf and Härtel edition), with a view of discovering any little misuses of slurs, I have failed in finding any which could not be logically accounted for; for example:

SONATA PATHETIQUE.

Beethoven's Way of Slurring.   *Alteration of several revised Editions.*

× The extension of the slur becomes correct, when in actual practice the final note is so shortened as to be equal to the previous one.

The extension of the slur is subject to the same condition as in the previous example.

We may, finally, accept the following principle:

The slur extension to a longer note than the last but one is correct, when the last note admits of being shortened to at least the equal duration of its preceding note. Where the last note does not admit of such shortening, the slurring is either wrong, or belongs to those exceptions which require a logical foundation.

EXCEPTIONS.

1. The first allowable case, where a slur may logically end with a much longer note than the preceding one, and where the final note is emphasized with a weighty, partly sustained touch, is the ending of a group with an *iambic* foot, ♩ ♩, ◡ —, which has already been explained.

Such an iambus, instead of appearing separately (as a group of two notes), may be adjoined to any number of preceding notes; these and the iambus forming together a slurred phrase of which the iambus is the terminating foot; for example:

BEETHOVEN—Sonata Appassionata, Op. 57.

The phrase ends with this iambus, ♩ ♩, which is instinctively executed, as here indicated, viz., with the insertion of a short break; and it would really be technically impossible to render the repetition, in octaves, otherwise.

All iambic phrase-endings are, of course, similarly treated in performance; for example:

CHOPIN—Nocturne, Op. 37, No. 1.

BEETHOVEN—Sonata, Op. 10, No. 3.

Iambic phrase-terminations occur as frequently in music as in poetry. They are the natural contrast to the more general trochaic endings, and justify many a phrase-slurring which would otherwise be a violation of the general rule.

2. The second exception is a sustained bass note, at the end of a descending passage, or phrase; for example:

CHOPIN—Ballade, Op. 23.

BEETHOVEN—Sonata, Op. 10, No. 3.

Such a bass note cannot be curtailed, for harmonic reasons.

This way of slurring, however, is not perfectly correct, although usage has made it legitimate. Yet it might be easily avoided, and so altered as to meet all requirements.

To prove this, I take the examples given above.

In Chopin's descending passage (as in other similar ones) the sustained bass note, at the end of the slur, is not really the terminating note of the phrase, but the initial note of a new (the next) phrase, and falling accidentally together with the final note of the previous phrase, as here exemplified:

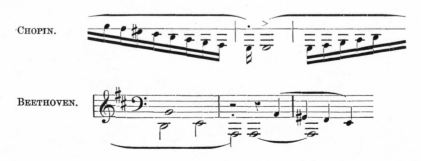

CHOPIN.

BEETHOVEN.

In orchestral or polyphonous music, such descending phrases would be terminated with a proportionately short note; while the sustained note, commencing the next phrase and falling together with the terminating note of the previous phrase, would be taken up by another voice or instrument. In pianoforte music, however, these two voices are drawn into one note, to save the trouble of writing two notes. This has become legitimate by long usage, but is, nevertheless, averse to the laws of slurring.

Looking upon the case from a strictly logical standpoint, there is no escaping from the fact, that, when a slur ends with a sustained note, the slurring is somewhere defective.

3. The third exception is accounted for by the ornaments of melody.

Musical ornamentation is, in one sense, the division of one (the main) note into a number of smaller ones; for example:

This note, ♪, is ornamented (or divided), thus :

" " ♪, " " " "

" " ♪, " " " "

Now, inasmuch as the total of ornamental notes represents, rhythmically, the value of the ornamented main note alone, the whole of such a group is really as much a unit as the one note originating the group.

When, therefore, a group of ornamental notes precedes the terminating note of a slur, the whole group may be considered as one note—one value.

The slurring thus receives a new scope of freedom, and yet Rule 3 is, logically, not violated.

According to this principle, terminations like the following may be considered as equalling the opposite ones.

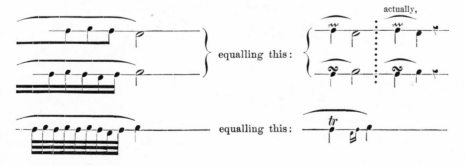

equalling this :

equalling this :

CHOPIN—Op. 27, No. 2.

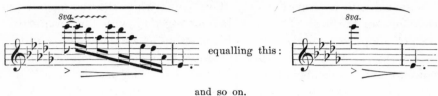

equalling this:

and so on.

Arpeggios may be counted as chords and, therefore, do not infringe the rules of slurring; for example:

CHOPIN—Ballade, Op. 47.

In cases, where the intervals of a chord are employed melodically, as in the following example:

CHOPIN—Ballad, Op. 23.

the intervals may also be considered as an *arpeggio*, or the slurring as falling under the last exception, viz., by taking the harmonic notes collectively, and considering this figure:

as being substantially this:

Notwithstanding exceptions, it is in every case, and always remains, a necessity to shorten the final note of all slurred groups sufficiently to produce a comprehensible break; because, without a break, a final note is not final, and there is no termination; and without a termination there is no phrasing.

CHAPTER VIII.

QUANTITATIVE ACCENTS.

THESE are as imperative and important as grammatical accents. They are, properly speaking, rhythmical, arising from the quantitative function of rhythm, as grammatical accents arise from its qualitative function. But I prefer to give them here under a melodic aspect, because, rhythmically, they are already covered, partly by positive grammatical, partly by syncopic accents.

The fundamental principle of quantitative accents arises out of the near and natural relation which exists between quantity and dynamics, or between duration and strength.

FIRST RULE.

Any note of longer duration than another requires dynamic preponderance (i. e., *accent*) *over the shorter note, in the same proportion that the duration of the longer note bears to the duration of the shorter one.*

In other words: *strength goes with length.*

The longer a note is, the more stress it requires.

On no other instrument is this principle so essential as on the pianoforte; for, to sustain a note on the pianoforte, it needs to be struck with sufficient force to cause it to vibrate the required length of time; and, as a matter of course, the longer the note is, the more forcibly it has to be struck.

---

1. *Accenting on quantity*—or length,
2. *Accenting on quality*—or strength,

are fundamental principles of accentuation. And, if we add

             3. *Accenting on extremes,*

and, as we see further on,

             4. *Accenting on dissonances,*

we have thus four fundamental principles of musical accentuation.

I might have classified accentuation as well, perhaps, according to these four principles, as in accordance with the four elements of music (rhythm, metric, melody, and harmony). But, having chosen the latter classification, and holding that to be, after all, the better one, I merely mention here the importance of these four fundamental principles, that they may be distinctly remembered as the basis of all accents.

Let us, now, see how this principle of accenting on quantity works in practice, and in connection with slurs.

Groups of Two Slurred Notes.

a. When two slurred notes are of the *same* value, the first note is always weightily accented, and the second note is shortened.

This rule holds good for both notes; it is immaterial, on what time-part they fall. For example:

BEETHOVEN—Sonata, Op. 14.

Positive Accents.

Negative Accents.

The slur denotes the accentuation; and a special sign, either of *forzando* (>) for the first, or of shortness (·) for the second note, is unnecessary.

b. When two slurred notes are of different values, the larger note is the accented one, and the smaller note is shortened; immaterial, which of the two notes comes first, or which comes last.

This is exemplified by the two opposite tact-feet—

The trochee, 𝆕 𝆕 , executed thus : 𝆕 𝆕 , and

The iambus, 𝆕 𝆕 , executed thus : 𝆕 𝆕 .

The shortening of a smaller note *before* a larger one is a new principle to us, as we have hitherto shortened final notes only.

This new principle is of far greater force and consequence than, at first sight, may be imagined.

Groups of Three Slurred Notes.

1. *When the three notes are of equal value*, quantitative considerations are not at all needed.

2. *When the three notes are of unequal value*, the chief stress belongs to the longest note.

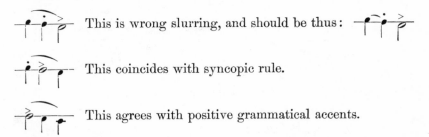

This is wrong slurring, and should be thus:

This coincides with syncopic rule.

This agrees with positive grammatical accents.

The principle of giving dynamic prominence to quantity applies chiefly to short groups of two or three notes, rarely to long groups.

In reference to the quality of quantitative accents, it has been stated, in substance, that the stress of any note is proportioned to the duration of the note.

A long note is a relative idea merely, inasmuch as even a short note

(𝅘𝅥𝅯) is long, when compared to a still shorter one (𝅘𝅥𝅰 or 𝅘𝅥𝅰).

Shorter, however, than any note is a rest, or silence.

Therefore, *any note coming after a rest is always long, compared to the preceding silence.*

From this arises another kind of quantitative accent, and hence the following rule.

SECOND RULE.

a. *Any note preceded by a rest is to be considered as a long note, and requires an accent.*

The quality of such an accent is proportioned to the value of the accented note; for example:

This rule opens an immense field for practical application, and requires no special illustration.

As a consequence of this rule follows this appendix:

b. *The note succeeding a slurred group is accented.*

The final note of a slur being shortened, the succeeding note is, virtually, preceded by a rest; for example:

Written.   *Executed.*

This gives again an endless variety of examples.

Another consequence of the rule is this:

c. *A repeated note is accented.*

Because a note, before being repeated, is shortened; for example:

Written.   *Executed.*

As it is, technically, impossible to strike the same note twice, without shortening the first one, the repeated note is thus actually preceded by a break or rest. It is from this fact, that all such cases are brought under the present rule.

In singing, also, this rule is naturally observed.

What numberless times have we heard this hackneyed opening phrase in Italian opera; for example:

and so on.

It is quite natural, that the oftener a note is repeated, the more the accent loses in force. In all quick repetitions on the pianoforte, as in Rosellen's sentimental "Reverie" and such like "Tremolos," the repetition notes cease altogether to be accented in conformity with the rule.

The observance of the present rule necessitates many a break at the end of a slur, which, though generally self-suggesting, ought, nevertheless, to be clearly—at all events, correctly—indicated by the slurring; for example:

In accenting repeated notes, it should be remembered that *the shortening of the note preceding the accent is as important, and even more essential, than the accent itself;* for example:

CHOPIN—Concerto in E-Minor, Op. 11.

CHOPIN—Prelude, No. 11.

BEETHOVEN—Sonata, Op. 53.

The abbreviation of a note (before repeating it) differs greatly as to the degree of its shortening.

The degree of such shortening depends on tempo, and the abbreviation should agree with the rule of appoggiaturas, which says:

"*The slower the movement, the shorter should be the appoggiatura.*"

Adagio.   *Moderato.*   *Allegro con moto.*   *Presto.*

(E. D. Wagner—"*Musikalische Ornamentik.*")

Applying this rule of appoggiaturas to repetition notes, which is perfectly sound, we establish the maxim that

The note preceding its own repetition is always shortened more or less, correspondingly to the tempo being slow or fast.

But we can go still further.

The principle of abbreviation is evidently an essential principle of quantitative accentuation, as embodied in the following rule.

THIRD RULE.

A note preceding a longer note than itself, or preceding its own repetition, is shortened to about one-half its value.

This shortening is regulated by the tempo in such a way, that, the slower the movement, the more the note is to be shortened, and *vice versa ;* for example:

BEETHOVEN—SONATA, Op. 26.

BEETHOVEN—SONATA PATHETIQUE.

Such abbreviations are as necessary as they are historically correct.

They are in accordance with the precepts of the older masters, notably Bach, Händel, etc., and Von Bülow points them especially out in his edition of the Sonata Pathetique.

12

This rule has, however, the following exceptions :

The note preceding a longer one is not shortened, *i. e.*, there is no rest or break after it.

1. In all cases of appoggiaturas ; for example :

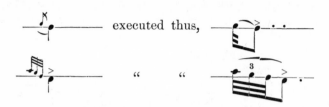

2. Or in any *legato* group in which the break, occasioned by the shortening of the last but one note, would be detrimental to the unity of the group and the desired *legato ;* for example :

As a general guidance, it may be stated that the rule has exclusively reference to two notes only, viz. : the shortened one and the succeeding longer note, with the object of making these two notes appear as an iambus, but not otherwise interfering with the unity of a *legato* group or phrase.

As to its application, I subjoin the following additional examples :

MOZART—Sonata in B-Flat.

THALBERG—Andante.

CHOPIN—BALLADE IN A-FLAT.

To better perceive the point I wish to convey through these examples, they should be compared with the original notation.

I have given only a few illustrations of quantitative accents; and the whole subject has been passed over more rapidly than its importance might seem to warrant. But, as its rules are so simple and their application so self-evident, I thought it unnecessary to add any further explanation.

Moreover, the subject of quantitative stress will be taken up again in the subsequent chapter of dynamics. But I feel bound to repeat here that quantitative stress, viz., the regulation of stress in touch, according to the quantity of the note—the proportioning of the one to the proportions of the other—is of the utmost significance to touch and musical accentuation in general, and to intellectual interpretation in particular.

PART IV.

HARMONIC ACCENTS.

INTRODUCTORY REMARKS.

HARMONY, in its most general significance, means Concord, Accord; and, in a narrower sense, simply " Chord."

Accepting this definition as the most appropriate for our purpose, we include in it the two opposite elements—

CONSONANCE AND DISSONANCE.

Consonance is " agreement ;" and dissonance, " disagreement." " The exact limit of consonance, or the point where dissonance begins, seems not definitely fixed, if fixed it can be. To define consonance to be agreeable sounds, and dissonance the reverse, as some do, is clearly absurd, because they both essentially belong to harmony or concord, or, as the Germans more properly call it, ' Die Kunst des Wohlklanges,' in which there can be nothing absolutely discordant."

The general significance of consonance, however, is confined to concording intervals; and that of dissonance, to discording intervals.

The concording (or consonating) intervals are:

Every octave, perfect fifth, perfect fourth, major and minor third, and major and minor sixth.

The discording (or dissonating) intervals are:

1. Every second, seventh, and ninth.

2. Every augmented and diminished interval.

Inasmuch as consonance and dissonance presuppose the simultaneous sound of two or more notes, it is evident, that, when either of these terms is applied to a single tone, it can only be in reference to the harmonic relation of that single tone; for, without such relation, a single tone is neither concording nor discording, but simply true or false (in pitch).

Chords are either consonant or dissonant.

They are consonant, when all the intervals are consonating among themselves, as well as collectively, counted from the bass note; for example:

A chord of three notes, to be consonant, must contain three consonant intervals; for example:

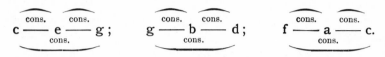

One of four notes must contain six consonating intervals; for example:

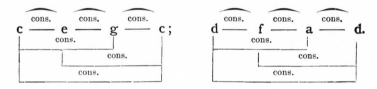

Chords are dissonant, if only one interval is dissonating; for example:

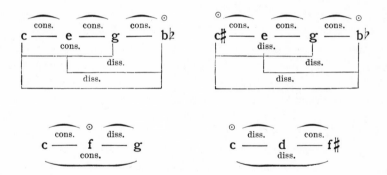

Although it takes two notes to constitute a dissonance, yet the dissonance is only one of the two, and appertains to that of the two notes which is not included in the fundamental concord.

The dissonance may be the upper note of the chord, or the middle, or the lower one (as indicated in the examples by an asterisk, ⊙).

Inasmuch as harmony consists of consonances and dissonances, it might be inferred that harmonic accents, likewise, would consist of consonant and dissonant accents; but such is not the case.

The two elements of harmony are not merely opposed to each other, as concord and discord, but are antagonistic also in other respects.

Consonance is not only " concord," " unity," " euphony," etc., but also " repose," " quiescence," " rest," and is—by nature—soft, gentle, peaceful.

Therefore, *consonance does not require to be made prominent by harmonic accent* (except where consonance appears dissonatingly).

Dissonance is not only " discord," dissent," " variance," etc., but also a " disturbance," " challenge,", " defiance," and—by nature—loud, energetic, contentious.

Hence, *dissonance demands to be made prominent by harmonic accent* (except when dissonance has no harmonic value, as in passing notes).

Consequently, we recognize only " accents of dissonances."

CHAPTER IX.

ACCENTS OF DISSONANCES.

"MANY theorists believe that the feeling of dissatisfaction, produced by the dissonances of music, arises from the mind not being able, without difficulty, to comprehend at once the arithmetical proportions of the vibrations. The foundation of dissonances, however, is generally allowed to be more æsthetical than intellectual. In music, dissonance may be called a necessary æsthetical evil, which is used for the purpose of producing pleasing contrasts with their resolutions."

A dissonance, in music, like a thorn in the flesh, is something foreign, which must be removed; like defiance, it is something aggressive, which must be appeased; something contentious, which must be transmuted into good understanding; something jarring, which must be euphonized.

In fact, a dissonance must be converted into a consonance; and this conversion is called, in musical parlance, " *resolving.*"

Resolving a dissonance means to cause it to progress by the nearest step (upward or downward) to a consonating note.

A *diatonical dissonance* is resolved diatonically the nearest step downward, which is either a tone or semitone.

A *chromatic dissonance* is resolved chromatically the nearest step upward or downward, which is always a semitone.

Diatonic dissonances are: every second, seventh, and ninth, in whatever diatonic scale; for example, in C-major:

In any of these intervals, it is either the upper or the lower note which dissonates. In either case, the dissonance is resolved the nearest diatonic step downward; for example:

The ninths are treated like the seconds.

Chromatic dissonances are more numerous. It is not necessary to enumerate these, and sufficient to state that any diatonical interval becomes a chromatic dissonance by being augmented (raised), or diminished (lowered). As this can only be done by an accidental (♯, ×, ♭, ♭♭, ♮), a chromatic dissonance is necessarily an accidental note (although not every accidental note is a dissonance).

The natural laws of resolving accidental intervals are these:

1. Any accidental sharp (♯) or double sharp (×) resolves upward, in continuation of its ascending tendency.

2. Any flat (♭) or double flat (♭♭) resolves downward, in continuation of its downward tendency.

3. A natural (♮) resolves either way.

a. In a scale with sharps, where it lowers, it follows its downward pulsion, by descending.

b. In a scale with flats, where it raises, it follows its upward drift, by ascending.

There are, however, exceptional cases when accidentals are not necessarily so resolved.   These are the following:

1. When an accidental is a consonance.

2. When more than one accidental occurs in dissonant chords; for example, in the chord of the diminished seventh, where only one of the accidentals is regularly resolved (upward), while the other may proceed either way; for example:

3. When an accidental is interchanged from one voice to another, it is sufficient, that the last-coming dissonance is regularly resolved.

HENSELT.

4. When the same dissonating note occurs in more than one harmonic part simultaneously, only one of the dissonating notes resolves regularly, while the other one proceeds in an opposite direction.

5. In dissonating sequences, or sequences of dissonances which will be explained under " Anticipation," further on; for example:

Without accidentals, a composition would remain in the same key, while the introduction of an accidental is the advent of one of three things.

1. The accidental note may be merely an accessory (passing) note of no harmonic value.

2. Or, through the accidental a direct change may occur into another consonant chord, when the accidental is a consonance.

3. Or, the accidental may effect a modulation, when it is a dissonance, specifically a modulating dissonance; virtually, a leading note, a sort of bridge from one diatonic to the next over the intervening semitone. For example:

An accidental C♯ is the leading or modulating note to D,
"   "   C♭   "   "   "   "   to B♭, etc.

With the hope of explaining all this more clearly, I give a practical illustration pointing out the progression of every dissonance and accidental note therein.

BEETHOVEN—Sonata, Op. 27, No. 2.

1. Diatonic dissonance. Seventh, dissonating with the key-note C-sharp ; descends.

2. Consonance. Key-note of D-major.

3. Consonance. Major third, ascends.

4. Diatonic dissonance. Seventh, descends.

5. Diatonic dissonance. Retardation of the previous C-sharp ; dissonates as lower second with D-sharp, resolves downward to B-sharp.

6. Consonance. (The chord being G-sharp, B-sharp, D-sharp.)

7. Diatonic dissonance. Seventh, descends.

8. Consonance. Major third, ascends.

9. Diatonic dissonance. Seventh of the key-note G-sharp, descends in next measure.

1. Diatonic dissonance. Seventh, descends.

2. Consonance. Direct change from E-major to E-minor.

3. The key being E-minor, this D is a consonance belonging to the G-major chord.

4. Diatonic dissonance. Seventh, descends.

5 and 6. Consonance.

7. Consonance, according to notation ; but, a diatonic dissonance (seventh), if the notation is erroneous. (See 8.)

8. This B-natural was probably an engraver's fault originally, and, very strangely, has never been rectified in any edition. There is no reason why the previous C-nat. should descend to this B, and form octaves with the bass; while it would be altogether more Beethoven-like if the C remained, and then ascended to the next C-sharp.

9. Chromatic dissonance. Ground-note of diminished septime chord, A-sharp, C-sharp, E, G ; becomes a major third (or leading-note) in the last quarter of the measure, and then ascends.

10. Chromatic dissonance. Diminished seventh, descends.

11. Consonance.

12. Consonance. Key-note of dominant septime chord, F-sharp, A-sharp, C-sharp, F.

13. Diatonic dissonance. Seventh, descends.

1. Consonance. Minor third.

2. Consonance. (Minor third) having a strongly dissonating effect because, dissonating with the C-sharp, it naturally resolves downward (following its tendency). (See 4.)

3. Consonance. Perfect fifth, but dissonating (as lower second) with the C-sharp; it resolves downward.

4. Interchange between treble and bass (see 2). As a lowered sharp, this chromatic interval follows its downward tendency by descending.

5. Consonance.

6. Consonance. Direct change from minor to major.

7. Chromatic dissonance. Ninth, descends.

8 and 9. Consonances.

10. Chromatic dissonance. Ascends. (This is an accessory note, or a free suspension —interposed between the previous C-natural and its resolution B.)

11. Consonance.

The dissonances in the next measure are repetitions of 7, 8, 9, 10, and 11.

It is not necessary to proceed further with this illustration; for, by taking up at random any piece of music, and examining the progression of dissonances—notably of accidental notes—the same principles as the foregoing will be found to prevail; viz.: that every diatonic dissonance descends, and every chromatic dissonance either descends or ascends, according to the tendency of the accidental.

Returning, now, to the accents of dissonances, I commence with the general rule—

Every dissonance should be accented.

This rule is not so simple as it appears; because not every discording interval is a harmonic dissonance. Therefore, the question arises: What is really a harmonic dissonance?

In modern music, dissonance is divided into *essential* (harmonic) and *accidental* (melodic); the former arising fundamentally; the latter, from passing notes, anticipations, etc.

Therefore, to make the rule more definite, it should be modified, thus:

RULE ONE.

Every harmonic dissonance should be accented, whereas melodic dissonances are to be passed over unaccented.

It now remains to be shown what constitutes a harmonic, and what, a melodic dissonance.

1. Melodic Dissonances, or Accessory Notes.

1. NEIGHBORING NOTES.......... $\begin{cases} a. & \text{Regular.} \\ b. & \text{Irregular.} \end{cases}$

2. PASSING NOTES. .... $\begin{cases} a. & \text{Regular.} \\ b. & \text{Irregular.} \end{cases}$

2. Harmonic Dissonances.

1. ANTICIPATIONS.

2. RETARDATIONS................. $\begin{cases} a. & \text{Prepared—Strict.} \\ b. & \text{Unprepared—Free.} \end{cases}$

3. MODULATING NOTES.

4. ORGAN POINTS.

The accentuation will be explained, as we go along.

CHAPTER X.

MELODIC DISSONANCES.

THESE have the general name of *Accessory notes.*

Accessory notes are all transitory, non-harmonic notes which enrich and ornament the melodic parts of the composition; for example:

WEBER.

The notes marked × are accessory ones, melodic dissonances of no harmonic value, and to be passed over lightly.

Accessory notes are of two kinds; either they stand *beside* a harmonic note, as in an appoggiatura, ————; or a trill, ————; or a turn, ————; or they lie *between two* harmonic tones, as in a scale:

In the former case, they bear relation to only one harmonic tone; we call these neighboring notes (or tones).

In the latter case, they bear relation to two harmonic tones; we call these passing notes.

Both neighboring and passing notes have again this distinction, that, when occurring on a weak time-part, they are regular transitions; and when happening on a strong time-part, they are irregular transitions.

Although, and just because accessory notes have no harmonic value, they are indispensable in melodic figuration, in filling in, and softening harmonic steps. They enable a composer to give a number of successive notes to a single sustaining chord, whereas, without them, each melodic note would require a separate chord.

They are employed in any one of the harmonic parts (soprano, alto, tenor, or bass), in melody or accompaniment; diatonically or chromatically; on a strong or weak time-part; in fact, they may occur anywhere and everywhere.

Let us, now, examine each special kind of accessory notes.

1. Regular Neighboring Notes.

Germ. *Neben-Noten.* Fr. *Notes voisines.*

The function of these is, especially, that of embellishment, and also to bring greater activity and flow into the melodic parts.

A neighboring note is always the nearest note to the tone which it embellishes. The latter we call the main tone.

The nearest note is, of course, the second, which may be the upper or lower second, either diatonic or chromatic; for example:

The C is here the main tone which is being embellished, the D being the upper, and the B the lower neighboring note; both being diatonic ones.

This A is here the main tone; this B-flat the upper, and the G-sharp the lower neighboring note; both being chromatic ones.

A diatonic neighboring note may be a whole or a half tone distant from its main tone; a chromatic one can only be a semitone from it.

The musical notation, or, so to say, the spelling of chromatic neighboring notes, should be in accordance with the rules of resolving accidentals, and avoid wrong progression; for example:

A neighboring note may appear freely before, or after, its main note, but must always go back to it, so that the main note is the last. This returning need not follow directly, as another neighboring note, or another main note, may be interposed ; for example :

If both the upper and lower seconds are employed, the embellishment becomes, of course, richer ; for example :

This leads already to great variety of combinations. More elaborate employment of such notes produces the usual musical ornamentation (Germ. *Manieren*, Fr. *Agréments*), such as, " the turn," " mordent," " trill," etc., which it is unneccessary to exemplify.

2. Irregular Neighboring Notes.

Germ. *Wechsel-Noten.*

All that has just been said about regular, applies equally to the irregular neighboring notes. The only difference being that the former occur on a weak part of of measure, whereas the latter happen on a strong part.

Further explanation needs but a few illustrations.

WEBER—First Sonata.

All the accented notes are here irregular neighboring notes.

Weber was very partial to, and much blamed for, his too frequent employment of such "Wechsel-Noten," as the Germans call them.

BEETHOVEN—SONATA, Op. 49.

The accents on such neighboring notes are due, for several reasons:

1. *Grammatically*—because the notes fall on strong time-parts.
2. *Melodically*—on account of the slur.
3. *Harmonically* (as we shall see further on)—on account of "the free suspensions"—"retardation"—"Vorhalt."

3. Regular Passing Notes.

Germ. *Durchgangs-Noten.* Fr. *Notes de passage.* Lat. *Transitus regularis.*

The step from one harmonic tone to another through intermediate non-harmonic notes is termed "transition" (Lat. *transitus*). The intermediate notes are called "transient" or "passing notes." In other words: a passing note is the neighboring note of two different tones between which it lies.

They are diatonical and chromatical.

Supposing the C-major chord to be the underlying harmony of a chromatic scale,

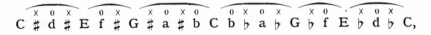

the notes marked × would be chromatic passing notes; those marked o, diatonic ones.

A change of key naturally effects a change in the diatonic and chromatic character of the passing notes.

Correct spelling is here as necessary as in neighboring notes; for example:

In the good old time when counterpoint reigned supreme, unprepared, non-harmonic notes, *i. e.*, freely introduced dissonances, were permitted only on a weak time-part. Such dissonances were called " passing notes " (Durchgangs-Noten), in opposition to the notes on the strong time-parts, which were called " accented notes."

The term " transitory " was not applied to all non-harmonic notes, without taking into account the time-parts they occurred on ; but, in order to make a distinction, those occuring on a weak time-part were termed *transitus regularis ;* and those on a strong part, *transitus irregularis.*

Some theorists consider as " transitory " every melodic note which has no harmonic value, on the ground, that such notes progress always to the main note; immaterial, whether they bear relation to only one main note, as the neighboring ; or to two, as the passing note. Originally, however, the name " passing note " signified the intermediate tone, in stepping from one tone to another higher or lower one. This is the narrower significance of the term, which most modern theorists accept as the correct one ; and it is in this sense, that I have dealt with the subject.

The recognition of passing notes is so simple and easy a matter as to require no further explanation.

A few illustrations may, however, not be amiss.

DUSSEK—*Diatonic Regular Passing Notes.*

O = diatonic regular passing notes.

BEETHOVEN—*Chromatic Regular Passing Notes.*

The notes, marked " o," are diatonic; those, marked " ×," chromatic passing notes.

4. Irregular Passing Notes.

Germ. *Wechsel-Noten.*   Fr. *Notes de passage.*   Lat. *Transitus irregularis.*
Ital. *Note Cambiata.*

In strict (Palestrina) style of counterpoint, dissonances on a strong time-part had to be prepared by being held over from a previous consonance; for example:

A freely introduced dissonance, however, was conceded under certain conditions and termed "Note Cambiata," or simply, "Cambiata" (the verb of which signified " to change," Germ. wechseln—hence the German term).

The concession of such a free dissonance arose from the circumstance, that it was thought unmelodical, in one-voiced chanting, to sing downward the interval of a fourth. To avoid and soften this step, another interval was interposed; and it was considered more melodious, that this should be the second, than the third; thus,

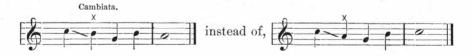

instead of,

This principle was retained in two and more voiced counterpoint, and considered as obligatory, until the eighteenth century, when, with the freer modern (Bach) style, this and many other restrictions disappeared. The term "Cambiata" is now obsolete, its former significance having passed away. Dissonances may now appear freely on any part of the measure.

All that has been said, regarding regular passing notes, applies equally to irregular ones; the difference being merely the time-part they fall on.

MOZART—SONATA IN C.

MOZART—SONATA IN C.

* (1)
* (2)
Seventh.
Seventh.

The notes, marked O, are regular; those, marked ×, irregular passing notes. The notes, marked *, are also passing; in substance thus:

* (1)

* (2)

Further on, we shall see that irregular passing notes and free retardations are identical.

Now, with regard to accentuation.

It is evident, that all melodic dissonances (falling on a weak time-part), viz., all regular accessory notes, whether neighboring or passing, should be passed over lightly and unaccented; whereas the irregular ones (falling on a strong time-part) are accented both grammatically and harmonically.

The harmonic emphasis required on the latter kind of notes is of great moment, and will be especially dealt with by-and-by under Retardation.

CHAPTER XI.

HARMONIC DISSONANCES.—ANTICIPATION AND RETARDATION.

ANTICIPATION (Germ. *Vorausnahme,* Fr. *contre-temps*) signifies the *anticipated* entrance of one, two, or more intervals, *before* the chord to which they belong. Any interval of a chord, introduced in advance of the chord, being an anticipation.

Anticipation differs from syncopation in this only, that the former is harmonical; the latter, rhythmical. In fact,

> *Anticipation* is harmonic syncopation;
> *Syncopation*, rhythmical anticipation.

The French term *contre-temps* refers to the rhythmical meaning; the German term *Vorausnahme,* to the harmonic meaning. *Retardation*— Germ. *Vorhalt,* Engl. *suspension*—is the *retarded* entrance of one, two, or more intervals, *after* the chord to which they belong.

Retardation refers both to harmony and to *tempo.*

With the latter significance (*ritardando*) we have, at present, nothing to do.

In the former sense, the Germans call retardation "Vor-halt," *i. e.,* holding before a chord an interval belonging to a previous chord.

They also use the term "Nach-halt," *i. e.,* holding after a chord an interval belonging to it.

These two terms are often confusing, because, though apparently of contrary meaning, they express virtually the same thing.

(Those who are German scholars should not confound "Vorhalt"— retardation, with "Vorschlag"—appoggiatura; the latter being simply an unaccented accessory note, whereas the former is accented.)

Bearing in mind that anticipation *precedes,* and retardation *follows,* the chord to which they belong, I repeat a few examples already given under Syncopation, in illustration of both.

BEETHOVEN—SONATA, Op. 27, No. 2.

The melody is here in harmonic anticipation with the bass.

SCHUMANN—DAVIDSBUNDLER.

(1) Anticipation.   (2) Retardation.

The melody is here both in retardation and in anticipation with the bass, or in either alone. This explains how the German terms, " Vorhalt " and " Nachhalt," may be confounded.

Anticipation is frequently an embellishment, merely for the purpose of introducing a melodic note in a more indicatory manner; for example:

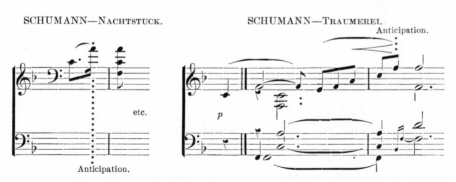

SCHUMANN—NACHTSTUCK.   SCHUMANN—TRAUMEREI.

Anticipations of this kind are shortened, on account of the note being repeated (quantitative accents), but are, of course, not accented.

Or, the melody is altogether anticipating the accompaniment, in this way:

SCHUMANN—The Merry Peasant.

SCHUMANN—First Loss.

The accentuation is here simply grammatical.

Anticipation also leads to many harmonic liberties, in the way of progression; for example, to sequences of septime chords.

a.

The above progression, without anticipation, would appear in its natural order, as follows:

b.

The notes in example *b*, marked by a cross (×), are the anticipated ones in example *a*.

Observe, also, the descending sharps in example *a*. Though appearing wrong, the order of succession is quite correct and logical when explained by the natural progression of example *b*.

Such kind of anticipated progression is frequently employed in modern compositions; for example:

CHOPIN—Ballade.

HENSELT—Etude.

Very little need be said regarding the accentuation.

Anticipations do not require to be harmonically accented. An anticipated note, when it is a consonance, has, as such, no harmonic prominence. When it is a dissonance, it is either melodical and transient, hence, passed over unaccented; or, it is harmonical, falling on a strong time-part (which is very rare), when its harmonic emphasis is entirely cast in the shade by other and stronger demands for accentuation, such as grammatical or syncopic.

Hence, we may say: anticipations are not harmonically accented.

It is different, however, with *retardations*. These are always accented.

Retardations or suspensions (these terms are synonymous) are either prepared, or unprepared.

Prepared suspensions are identical to what are termed, in counterpoint, "prepared dissonances."

To accent these is, of course, impossible, owing to the tie. The emphasis, however, is not omitted, but is anticipated by syncopic accent.

Unprepared suspensions, or freely introduced retardations (in German, "freie vorhalte"), are the strongest of dissonances.

This class of suspensions occurs in three ways—

1. *Melodically*, as an irregular passing note (wechsel-note); or, *harmonically*, gradually prepared, step-wise introduced, so to say; for example:

BEETHOVEN—Sonata, Op. 22.

DÖHLER—Nocturne.

The accent on such "step-wise" introduced dissonances is stronger on a chromatic (being a more strange) note, than on a diatonic one; but is less pronounced, less sharp than the stress demanded by the following kind of suspensions.

Or, the suspension happens—

2. *Melodically*, as an irregular neighboring note (wechsel-note); or, *harmonically*, totally unprepared, jumped into, so to say; for example:

RUBINSTEIN—Etude.

HILLER—Zur Guitarre.

The emphasis on totally unprepared suspensions is always of a more pronounced character than if the dissonance were partially prepared, as the foregoing kind.

3. Or, the suspension is anticipated (struck in advance), without being tied; for example, in this way:

HENSELT—Petite Valse.

MENDELSSOHN—Song without Words, No. 7.

This anticipation, however, does not soften the unexpectedness of the suspension, nor the force or intensity of its accent.   On the contrary, it rather adds to the emphasis; because, as the anticipated note has to be shortened, by reason of its being repeated; thus:

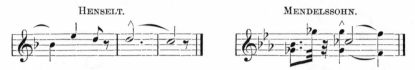

This causes the suspension following to be accented also, by reason of its greater length.   (See Quantitative Accents.)

Now, it is but logical, that, when accentuation is required on several grounds, the emphasis is stronger than if it were called for on one ground only.   And, as always in the case of unprepared (free) suspensions, several reasons unite to demand emphasis; for example:

> *Harmonically*—the dissonance;
> *Rhythmically*—the strong time-part;
> *Melodically*—the slur, or the quantity of the note, or both.

So is their accentuation not only, invariably, a very pronounced one, but there is hardly anything else in music which demands more imperatively dynamic prominence, than suspensions.   And suspensions, it must be remembered, are really the only kind of dissonances that are accented; as, *vice versa*, accented dissonance (excepting organ-points) is a suspension, or an irregular accessory note, which is the same thing.

Let us, now, suppose the student to be quite competent to recognize every kind of suspension, and, consequently, to know perfectly

WHEN AND WHERE

a dissonance ought, and ought not, to be accented.   Yet, this knowledge would not include the consciousness of

HOW

to give these accents.

Although "how to accent," as a general question, has already been declared inexplicable (page 24); yet, I think, it would be both interesting and beneficial to the reader to pause here, and investigate the difficulties which render a solution of the question—even in merely its special bearing on dissonances—impossible.

How to accent, apart from its emotional element, has a direct reference to

1. The quality, or dynamic stress, of the accented note;
2. The quantity, or rhythmical duration, of the accented note.

To determine merely the former, and simply in cases of dissonances, requires already the following considerations:

Harmonically, the dissonance itself; upon the principle, that the greater the dissonance the stronger should be the accent.

Grammatically, the time-part the dissonance falls on ; upon the principle, that strong time-parts are accented, and weak ones not.

Melodically, the position of the dissonance, viz., whether it is in the treble or bass, in an inner or outer voice, in an extreme or not extreme position, etc. ; upon the principle, that the accent is more important in the melody than the accompaniment, in an outer than an inner voice, at the climax of a *crescendo* than at the beginning of one, at the extreme of a passage than in the middle of it, etc.

Quantitatively, the duration of the accented note ; upon the principle, that the longer the duration the greater should be the stress of the accent.

Also the phrases, slurs, tempo, etc., must be considered.

Here already, from the outset, we are burdened and hampered by so many considerations, as to make it, apparently, impossible to arrive at any system by which to regulate the quality of accent.

To simplify the matter, however, most of these considerations may here be put aside; not only because they have been treated already, but because, in examining the accents of dissonances from a harmonic point, as we are doing, we may as well confine ourselves to harmonic reasons.

Therefore, I take into account the dissonance itself only, and make that alone the subject for investigation.

A dissonance is accented on harmonic grounds, simply because it is a discord (page 182).

Since this is sufficient cause to call for an accent, it stands to reason, that *the greater the discord, or the cause, the stronger should be the accent.*

If, therefore, we could set up a scale of dissonances, grading them according to their greater or less acuteness, we might then also establish a scale of accents corresponding to the scale of dissonances. But this is hardly possible to do, as we have no reliable standard by which to measure the acuteness of a dissonance. (We cannot even determine the point where dissonance begins and consonance ends.)

Supposing we made the ear the standard :

The result would be vastly different with different individuals.

One person would consider as more or less harsh a dissonance which another would think more or less mild. Or, the same dissonance, striking the ear unexpectedly and alone, would have quite another effect from that which it would produce, coming well prepared or covered by other sounds. The latter difference would be quite as great, as taking pepper alone, or taking it mixed in a dish.

Now, some people like pepper, and others do not.

It is the same with dissonances.

To establish a scale of the latter, according to the standard of the ear, is therefore simply impossible.

Supposing, then, we measured the acuteness of a dissonance by reasoning, and started from the hypothesis—

A dissonance is the greater the nearer it approaches a perfect consonance.

Yet we could not establish a scale upon it.

The above supposition, paradoxical as it may appear, is, nevertheless, quite correct; not only in music, but also in most conditions of life when applied in the sense of disagreement.

In music, the most perfect consonance is the octave or unison. Now, if two persons sang or gave on any instrument the same note in unison, or in the octave, and one of the two notes were out of pitch, then the nearer the dissonating note to the consonance, the greater, the more aggravating would be the dissonating effect.

In fact, *the harshest of all dissonances is an impure consonance.*

Without considering minute fractions of a tone, it is evident, that the nearest semitone to an octave or to a prime is more acute than any note further removed from the consonance.

And yet, the harshest of dissonating intervals—a major seventh and minor second—would strike the ear more naturally when well introduced, or covered by surrounding sounds, than a far less acute interval would do, when appearing unexpectedly. In the former case, the greater dissonance would actually be the smaller; in the latter, the smaller dissonance would virtually be the greater.

Hence, we cannot establish a scale upon either of these propositions.

And again, supposing we started from the principle, that *the more a dissonance is prepared, the less it is acute ; the more unprepared it appears, the more it is acute.*

This, being both rational and, to a certain extent, even practical, may be received as a general rule (probably the best that can be given); but, although this rule may be of some service, it is not sufficiently definite to establish upon it an approximate scale.

In fact, we are forced to the conclusion, that reason cannot invent, nor science discover, a reliable standard by which to measure the relative acuteness of dissonances. Hence, we cannot regulate the quality of their accents accordingly.

But there is yet another harmonic basis (instead of acuteness) to be examined, viz.: *the utility of dissonances.*

The utility consists in the dissonance being either a color-giving, piquancy conferring, harmonic contrast, or, in being the means of modulation, a connecting link or bridge from one harmony to another.

Now, whereas a dissonance, in its acuteness, is an antagonistic element in harmony; in its utility, it is the pith and quintessence of harmony, fulfilling a friendly aiding function.

Dissonances, then, are to be viewed from two aspects: from a positive side, *i. e.*, their utility, and from a negative side, *i. e.*, their acuteness.

Having before taken the negative side as a basis, we now try the positive side.

The utility of dissonances, as already stated, consists in—

1. The dissonance being a harmonic contrast, either

   a. One of beauty, or mellowness; for example:

HENSELT—Poëme d'Amour, Op. 3.

   b. Or one of expressive harshness; for example:

SCHUBERT—Am Meere.

   c. Or, in the dissonance being a modulating agent (see next chapter).

Mellowness and harshness, in harmonic respect, are relative ideas, merely depending on personal taste; and it is evident, that innumerable grades and shades exist between the softest and the harshest dissonance.

Having found it impossible to measure the acuteness of dissonances, it is, of course, still more impossible to define the finer grades and shades of harmonic contrasts. And, as the dynamic stress of harmonic accents must naturally correspond with the mellowness or harshness of harmonic contrast, we must, therefore, altogether relinquish the attempt of regulating or determining "how to accent," in reference to the *quality* of accents.

But we have not yet completed this investigation; for we have still to ascertain if it is not possible to arrive at some discrimination, in reference to the *quantity* of accents.

Regarding *quantity*, it has been laid down as a fundamental law of accentuation (page 40), that every musical accent must either be "sustained" or "shortened."

It may, now, further be stated, that this quantitative distinction is virtually all that can be subjected to rule and reasoning, both in the general question of "How to accent," and in the special question of "How to accent dissonances."

Such distinction is of considerable æsthetic importance, and a valuable adjunct of artistic musical expression.

It has already been shown that a dissonance must be resolved, and that the resolution terminates the dissonance. It is the same with suspensions. The resolution terminates the suspension.

Suspension and resolution ought, therefore, to be taken together as a unity; the latter being analogous, in music, to a dissyllabic word (or foot) in prosody.

Thus, a dissonance with its resolution forms either a musical *trochee*,

or a musical *iambus*,

Each of these two feet is the vehicle of almost the opposite emotion.

A trochee expresses something pathetic and deep—a sigh, or the pressure of emotion.

An iambus, on the other hand, expresses something joyful and light—an effusion of pleasure or lightheartedness.

Notice, for example, the difference of these two feet in a polonaise:

Iambus.

How joyful, brilliant, and bold this opening iambus appears, compared to the stateliness, intensity, and pathos of this terminal trochee:

The following illustrates a mixture of both these feet in a slow movement:

BEETHOVEN—Kreutzer Sonata.

Whatever doubt may be had, as to the iambic foot being gay or aspiring, it cannot be denied, that the trochaic foot is never gay, but always serious, pathetic, sighing.

The unity of a dissonance and its resolution represents, in most cases, a musical trochee.

Now, it should be borne in mind, for it is an important principle of expression, that, analogous to prosody, the two notes (or syllables) which form the trochee *should not be separated, but closely joined.*

Hence, the rule:

Every accented dissonance (or suspension) should be sustained and slurred over to its resolution.

Ample illustration of this rule will be found in the next chapter.

The reverse treatment, arising from the opposite or iambic foot; for example :

CHOPIN—Polonaise.

HUMMEL—Concerto (A-Minor).

This treatment, however, is really an exception merely, and occurs comparatively rarely.

Although the last rule does not tell us how to regulate the *quality* of an accented dissonance, yet it teaches us how to discriminate as to its *quantity*, viz., whether to mark the dissonance with a sustained emphasis, or with a short accent.

This is about the only rule which can be given on the subject of " How to accent."

As further attempts would inevitably prove futile, we now quit that subject.

Discrimination of touch in respect to strength is, by the bye, a subject altogether out of place here, but which will receive more especial attention under the subsequent chapter of dynamics.

CHAPTER XII.

MODULATING NOTES.

I DESIGNATE by this term certain accidental notes which, on account of their modulating function, require to be accented.

Referring to page 185, we find that in every composition " the introduction of an accidental is the advent of one of three things," viz. :

1. The accidental may be merely a melodic accessory note of no harmonic value.

2. Or, through the accidental a direct change may occur into another consonant chord, when the accidental is a consonance.

3. Or, the accidental may effect a modulation, when it is a dissonance ; virtually, a leading-note, a sort of bridge from one diatonic tone to the next, over the intervening semitone ; for example :

An accidental C$\sharp$ is the leading or modulating note to D,
"   "   C$\flat$ "   "   "   "   B$\flat$.

It is with the latter kind of accidentals we now have to deal.

In modulating from one key to another, it is only necessary to introduce euphoniously the dominant septime chord, or, simply, the leading note of the key into which one desires to modulate.

This leading note is, of course, an accidental (foreign to the scale), which to introduce is easy enough in transitions to near-related keys ; but which becomes difficult, requiring both ingenuity and experience, when modulating into distant keys.

How to do this, so as to avoid harshness, and cause the transition to fall naturally upon the ear, depends chiefly on the composer ; but also, in some measure, on the performer.

Especially in direct transition, where the softening interposition of modulation is wanting, the performer has to make the transition not only palatable, but attractive, by judicious phrasing.

Judicious phrasing demands complete separation, by a break, between the old and the new phrase. The old harmony (old phrase) should termi-

14

nate *ritardando;* the breath-taking pause (or break) between the old and
new phrase should be prolonged, in proportion to the strangeness of the
transition; and the new phrase should then begin *a tempo;* for example:

SCHUMANN—Faschingsschwank, Op. 26.

The phrase ends *ritard.* After a slight pause, the new phrase begins *a tempo.*

If the little "*rit.*" and the pause, "⌢," here suggested, were not observed, and the movement should be played on in time, the effect, instead
of being artistic, would be spoiled, and the interpretation would give evidence of immaturity or crude perception.

SCHUMANN—Arabesque, Op. 18.

Here, again, the performer can greatly soften the rather unexpected
transition by a preceding *ritardando* and a slight pause (⌢) on the D♯, just
before the double bar, ‖. This D♯, which is enharmonically carried over
as E♭, is the connecting link between the old and the new harmony. By
sustaining it, the transition becomes comprehensive, and the change of
key a pleasant surprise rather than a harsh one.

*The practice of retarding before, and pausing between, direct transi-
tions, is not only applicable, but necessary, in most cases of sudden
changes of key.*

On the other hand, when a modulating dissonance softens and prepares
the transition, the transition cannot be called a direct one, and a break is

not necessary. But the modulating note, which has been compared to a bridge, should be (like every bridge) a strong one, and therefore *must be clearly emphasized to call attention to the harmonic change.* Also, as an important desideratum, it is, in most cases, desirable *to sustain the accented dissonance until its resolution*, even when this is not indicated; for example:

SCHUMANN—FASCHINGSSCHWANK, Op. 26.

The accidental F♯, in the second measure, is here a modulating dissonance, leading to G-minor in the third measure. This F♯ is not only harmonically accented, but may actually be joined to its resolution G, so as to

produce this trochaic effect, 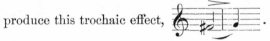 .

Such treatment, though not indicated, is both proper and logical; because it would be highly unsatisfactory, and certainly not euphonious, if the dissonance disappeared, evaporated, so to speak, before having reached its resolution.

Thus, the following principle may safely be accepted—

The sustaining of an accented dissonance (suspension or modulating note) until its resolution, whether indicated or not, is both desirable and proper, in every case where it is technically practicable, providing no interposing harmony holds the resolution in suspense.

For example:

MENDELSSOHN—SONG WITHOUT WORDS, No. 9.

Here, the sustaining of the modulating dissonance is indicated.

JENSEN—The Mill, Op. 17, No. 3.

Here, the carrying over of the C♯, in the bass, is not indicated in the original.

When the sustaining of a modulating dissonance is technically impossible, the modulating note should, at least, be strongly emphasized, so as to make it clearly perceptible; for example:

BEETHOVEN—Sonata, Op. 53.

A. *Written.*   B. *Harmonic Effect.*

Under *A*, where the leading dissonances cannot be sustained, the harmonic basis, as under *B*, should be borne in mind, and an approximate effect aimed at, through accentuation.

Cases, like the above, occur in great numbers, but are far more frequently overlooked than attended to.

BEETHOVEN—Sonata, Op. 53.

Attention is here called to the C-flat and D-flat, under the two asterisks (✱). In the Bülow edition of this sonata, these two points are considered as imitations, and a foot-note says:

"The imitations in the first and second voice are to be brought out by special accentuation."

Fully recognizing these points as imitations, I ascribe to them additional and greater importance as modulating notes. In this view, I do not only accent them, but sustain and slur them over to their resolution; thus:

With this trochaic effect:

This effect overshadows even the indicated *sforzando* or the real leading notes, D-natural and E-natural. It is true, Beethoven did not prescribe such treatment, but, the reasons being logical, and the effect gratifying, any one, excepting a pedant, should find therein sufficient justification for a liberty not nearly as great as would be freely accorded to any vocalist.

Very frequently, the accidentals which occur in a bass-part or an inner voice bear no indication of either emphasis or sustaining. But this should not hinder the interpreter from both emphasizing and sustaining the accidental dissonance, until its resolution is reached; for example:

CHOPIN—ÉTUDE, Op. 25, No. 2.

The notation of the two separate little phrases (a small sample of the thoroughness of Klindworth's edition of Chopin),

is not to be found in the original version, but is decidedly an improvement, because it calls attention to points that are generally overlooked.

BEETHOVEN—SONATA PATHETIQUE.

A similar example, in which the *crescendo* and accentuation of the modulating accidentals in the bass (here passing notes) are not indicated in the original edition.

It is, of course, impossible to give examples of all the instances in which accidentals are to be, or are not to be, accented. The only guidance is the dissonating character of the accidental, viz., the accidental being accented when it affects the harmony dissonatingly, and not accented when the harmony is left unaffected by it.

Finally, the student should bear in mind that all accented dissonances are either *suspensions* (retardations) and, as such, irregular neighboring notes, which resolve into their main note, and form, together with the latter, a dissyllabic foot, viz., either a trochee or an iambus; or they are *modulating notes* and, as such, irregular passing notes, which, together with the previous and terminating note, form a trisyllabic foot, having the accent on the middle syllable, as in the classic *amphibrachys*, exemplified by the

word "*So - nā - ta,*" in music, thus :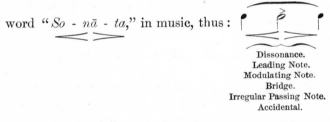

Dissonance.
Leading Note.
Modulating Note.
Bridge.
Irregular Passing Note.
Accidental.

ORGAN-POINTS.

The term "organ-point" signifies a sustained ground-bass (either the tonic or dominant), upon which a cadenza is formed of different chords or harmonies, which may or may not accord with the organ-point; for example:

BACH—GAVOTTE. Arranged by SAINT-SAENS.

The term is also employed to designate any sustained note (Germ. *liegende Stimme*) which may occur in any one of the harmonic parts, in the soprano, alto, tenor, or bass.

In organ playing, any sustained note (*liegende Stimme*) is simply struck without being accented, the tone retaining its volume by merely being held down. In pianoforte playing, however, a sustained tone cannot be made to retain its volume, but inevitably becomes weaker every moment. Therefore, quantitative accentuation has to be called into requisition to give a sufficiently strong impetus to the vibration of the strings, so as to sustain the tone as long as possible.

This accentuation of organ-points can hardly be considered as being called for on harmonic ground, but rather on quantitative principles. We may, therefore, pass over these organ-points, without any further explanation or exemplifying.

But there is another kind of organ-point, occurring in pianoforte music exclusively, which, on account of its extending over a number of measures, cannot be sustained and, therefore, has to be repeated, *i. e.*, struck over again.

This, it may be desirable, to point out by a few examples:

CHOPIN—POLONAISE IN A-FLAT, Op. 53.

The Organ-point is here D in the Tenor, during six measures. | And here, E-flat in the Tenor.

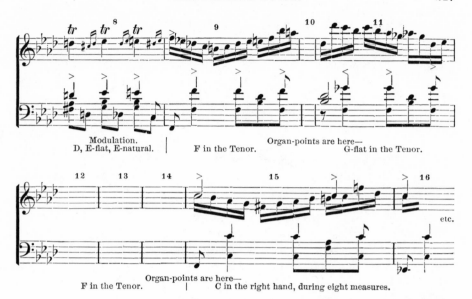

Modulation.
D, E-flat, E-natural. | F in the Tenor. Organ-points are here— G-flat in the Tenor.

F in the Tenor. Organ-points are here— | C in the right hand, during eight measures.

CHOPIN—POLONAISE IN F-SHARP MINOR, Op. 44.

The organ-point is here the A in both hands, during nineteen measures. This is followed by an eight-measured period, containing the chief theme, after which the same organ-point on A is repeated during sixteen measures, with harmonic variations; and then the second movement, *tempo di mazurka*, commences.

It is with these organ-points as with most accents; proper recognition precedes actual execution, and is the chief requirement of correct interpretation.

PART V.

DYNAMICS.

INTRODUCTORY REMARKS.

DYNAMICS (from the Greek; δύναμις, power,) "is that division of mechanics which contains the doctrines of the motion of bodies produced by force." In a wider sense, "the science which investigates the action of force." Applied to music, it refers to, and is understood to impart, the power or intensity of sounds.

"He is master of the dynamics of music who knows how to give to each and every sound that power which the subject requires, including the soft and loud, the *crescendo* and *diminuendo*, the abrupt and gentle, and every other possible variety."

There are five principal dynamic degrees:

1. *Pianissimo,*   3. *Mezzoforte,*
2. *Piano,*   4. *Forte,*
                5. *Fortissimo,*

and six dynamic tones:

1. *The organ-tone,* symbolized thus: ‗‗‗‗, which commences, continues, and ends with equal degree of power.

2. *The crescendo,* ◁‗‗, commencing soft, and gradually increasing.

3. *The diminuendo,* ‗‗▷, commencing loud, and gradually decreasing.

4. *The swell* (or *espressivo*), ◁ ▷, which is a union of *cresc.* and *dimin.*

5. *The pressure-tone* (or sustained accent), <, which is a very sudden *crescendo.*

6. *The explosive tone* (or short accent), >, which is an instantaneous *diminuendo.*

That each of the five dynamic degrees is a relative idea merely, is evident, from the fact that science has not as yet discovered the means of measuring definitely the power of sounds. It is, therefore, impossible to specify positively the exact limit of what is *forte*, or what is *piano*.

This inability, however, is not to be regarded. On the contrary, by leaving a wide range for individuality, it enables even delicately organized or physically weak pianists to attempt playing compositions requiring great power, which, otherwise, would be beyond their reach; and to play such pieces as well and effectively, though not as loudly, as other, more robust, pianists.

The great point, in dynamic respect, to be aimed at, without which no pianist can be an artist, is not so much the attainment of immense power, but that of having one's touch under such perfect control as to be able to say:

This is my *pianissimo;* this, my *piano;* my *mezzoforte;* my *forte;* my *fortissimo.*

Such discrimination of touch, when judiciously applied, converts mere mechanism into artistic technique, and is not only of far greater moment than the most marvelous execution without such discrimination, but contains the true charm of pianoforte playing, the secret of success, such as execution alone could never attain. In fact, the proper application of dynamic degrees and tones constitutes *the beauty of musical expression.*

We have enumerated five dynamic degrees and six tones. Regarding the latter, it must be mentioned that, in pianofore playing, the organ-tone, the *crescendo*, the *diminuendo*, and the swell, can only be produced on a succession or a plurality of notes. Without discussing whether the term " tone," applied to a plurality of notes, is a fit one or not, we simply accept it, for want of a better term.

But, by thus applying the idea of dynamic tone to a succession of notes, we find that two of the six dynamic tones may be dispensed with, viz. :

1. The *organ-tone*, which is not only impossible, but, on account of its continued sameness, undesirable, in pianoforte playing.

2. The *swell*, which does not consist of one, but, really, of two dynamic tones.

This leaves us only four dynamic tones in pianoforte-playing, re-enumerated, thus:

1. The *crescendo*, ⎯⎯⎯⎯⎯.
2. The *diminuendo*, ⎯⎯⎯⎯⎯.
3. The sustained accent, ⎯< or ∧.
4. The short accent, ⎯> or ʼ.

Regarding the five degrees, it has been mentioned, that they are rela-tive merely—in other words, proportioned to each other. When, therefore, the exact power of one degree is ascertained, it should be comparatively easy to find the others.

As a mariner can tell every point of the compass by knowing one of its points, the north; so, a pianist should be able to determine every degree of his strength by knowing one of its degrees—that of his extreme *fortissimo*.

When sure of this extreme point, a pianist can then, by his intelligence, direct the mechanism of touch so as to grade the other dynamic degrees, from this point downward, to the softest *pianissimo*.

Let us suppose that a pianist has correctly determined what is to be his *fortissimo*, his *forte*, his *piano*, etc., and that his touch responds unfailingly to this intellectual arrangement: now, the question arises, *when* and *where* is he to employ each particular degree, including the *crescendo* and *dimi-nuendo*, the abrupt and gentle, and every other dynamic discrimination.

Our first step in systematizing the *accents* of music was to classify them according to the four elements of music. This classification, how-ever, cannot be applied to dynamics, because—

The theory of musical dynamics has to do with melody alone.

Although the other elements call for accent (which is a dynamic tone), yet, the degree of power of every accent is regulated by the proportionate power of melody; the latter being really the lawgiver.

Melody, beside being the only musical element which requires the other dynamic distinctions, *crescendo* and *diminuendo*, etc., as well as ac-cents, is, moreover, that element which governs and determines the proper degree of force of every musical sound.

In fact, we have to consider the dynamic power of the tones of melody as the normal power; and, consequently, that all dynamic discrimination starts from, and is relative to, this normal degree.

Accepting this statement as a leading principle, we base upon it the principles of dynamic discrimination.

CHAPTER XIII.

THE DYNAMICS OF MELODY.—MELODY UNACCOMPANIED.

SIMPLE melody, in music, is like a nude figure in painting. Both require the touch of a master, and need a truer, purer conception as well as execution than if the melody were clothed in harmony, or the figure in drapery.

Many a painter excels in painting gorgeous draperies; or pianist, in playing elaborate accompaniments—each so gorgeous, or so elaborate, that the subject itself seems to hold but a secondary rank. But few artists approach the perfection which is needed in unadorned form or simple tune. The true artist, only, can hope to paint the nude in classic purity— the finished pianist, only, can expect to play a plain melody with dynamic perfection.

The intelligent playing of an unaccompanied melody is, dynamically, almost entirely a question of accentuation, with the addition only of *crescendo* and *diminuendo*, and sudden dynamic changes.

The first thing to be considered is the opening degree of power of the melody.

As the opening degree progresses, its intensity rises above, or falls below, that of the opening degree. But the opening degree is really the normal, or rule-giving, proportion of power, to which the subsequent degrees are merely relative.

As no positive rule can be laid down, in reference to what is *forte*, or *piano*, etc., great latitude must be allowed to individuality, and each performer must himself decide upon the exact degree of power with which the melody begins, according to his own conception of what is *forte*, or what *piano*, etc.

Unaccompanied melody does not really belong to the province of the pianist, and, except as a contrast, is hardly suitable to his instrument.

Even those solo melodies which are most suggestive of emotion, and almost self-expressive, so to speak, can only be inadequately rendered on a piano-forte, although the interpretation be masterly; for example:

Could any pianist, however great, draw from his instrument such ten-der tones, and produce such a deep impression, as a good violoncellist could do, in playing these measures?

Surely not.

But, the moment the melody is accompanied, the piano can hold its own. Take, for example, the recitative in the *larghetto* of Chopin's F-minor Concerto. Could any other instrumentalist surpass, or even equal, the pianist, in rendering this recitative with orchestral accompani-ment?

I think not.

But the real sphere for pianoforte music is certainly " polyphony."

MELODY ACCOMPANIED.

Polyphony is the proper domain of the pianist, the realm in which he is supreme, and in which no other instrumentalist, not even the organist, can compare with him.

The organist, with all his great advantages, yet lacks many of the facilities and most of the finer *nuances* of the pianist, notably that of accentuation, instantaneous dynamic, discrimination through touch, and that most important condition of expression—*pulsation*.

Without further comparisons, we will now examine what the pianist is able and expected to do, in dynamic respects.

In the study of accents, we had to do with dynamic distinctions of single notes only, or with special points. Here, however, leaving aside accentuation, we have to deal with dynamic distinctions of whole series of notes, or with collective points.

The series of notes which, collectively taken, require dynamic consideration, viz., each a distinctly different power, are :

> 1. MELODY;
> 2. FUNDAMENTAL BASSES;
> 3. ACCOMPANIMENTS.

Melody and basses, like the outlines of a picture, should be plainly perceptible, and the accompaniment, or inner voices, subdued.

The proportion which these different powers bear to each other is, as follows :

1. Melody, being the principal constituent of a composition, invariably demands primary power.

2. The fundamental basses, coming next in importance, claim secondary power.

3. The accompaniment, as the general servant, should be kept in the background and receive the least, or tertiary, power.

Accepting these proportions as the rule, we shall see by illustrations how this rule works in practice.

a. Plain Melody, with Simple Accompaniment.

DÖHLER—NOCTURNE.

Theoretically, it is easy enough to say: Give to the melody primary power; to the basses, secondary; and to the accompaniment, tertiary; practically, however, this is not quite so easy, for technical reasons. But, leaving technique aside, there still remains the intellectual difficulty of properly *locating* each voice, hence each dynamic power.

Although this presents no difficulty whatever in simple cases like the last examples, where the melody is unmistakable; yet, when the leading melody is doubtful or hidden, as happens frequently, its discernment assumes the proportion of an intellectual task which to solve correctly not every pianist is sufficiently thoughtful or capable.

b. **Plainly discernible Melody, with Complicated Accompaniment.**

MENDELSSOHN—LISZT—Wedding-march.

The consciousness of what is melody, and what is not, in the thousands of instances like the above, may be very plain to the performer; and yet the melody may not be at all clear to the listener. Abstracting again technique from our consideration, and allowing technique to be correct, the fault is generally intellectual, specifically a dynamic one. Not that the melody has been played too softly (for it may even be pounded, without making it clear); but that the accompanying flourishes have been played too loudly—that was the fault.

No passage or embellishment around a *canto* can ever be in good taste or of good effect, unless they are played in subdued proportion to the melody. They should be transparent as trelliswork, delicate as arabesques, —an ornament, not an encumbrance. This is a maxim universally accepted, the gist of which holds always good, even in *fortissimo* playing.

In fact, I may lay down this other rule:

No passage or flourish should be played fortissimo, *i. e., with the performer's greatest power, unless it occurs alone, and cannot drown another voice of superior importance.*

Playing brilliant accompaniments in subdued proportion to the melody need not, by any means, be a sign of weakness or effeminacy, nor need such accompaniment remain within the limit of *piano;* but they should never arrogate a prominence which does not belong to accompaniments.

15

c. Not plainly discernible Melodies.

Of these I distinguish two kinds:

1. Those which are evidently intended by the composer as melodies.

2. Those about which it is doubtful whether the composer premeditated them as melodies.

FIRST KIND.

The following are a few examples:

SCHUMANN—Novelette, No. 2.

The melody, being somewhat obscured by the change of hands, is evidently intended to be thus:

When so recognized, primary power can then be correctly located.

TSCHAÏKOWSKY—Barcarolle, Op. 37, No. 6.

Unencumbered, the melody would appear thus:

and this would be the response:

etc.

Although these few examples are naturally inadequate to illustrate the numerous cases in which the melody is so obscured that it is not readily discerned by the ordinary reader, yet they prove sufficiently the necessity of searching for, and finding, the melody, before bringing into play dynamic discrimination.

SECOND KIND.

Hidden melodies about which it is doubtful whether the composer premeditated them.

CZERNY—L'Ecole de la Velocité, No. 15.

Melody.

BEETHOVEN—Sonata, Op. 53.

BEETHOVEN—Sonata, Op. 53.

CHOPIN—ALLEGRO DE CONCERT.

Such kind of bass melody is very frequent in Chopin.

CHOPIN—Etude, Op. 10, No. 5.

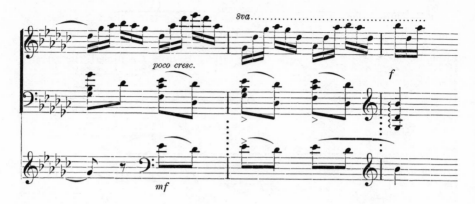

Whether the composer intended such hidden melodies, or not, should never deter the performer from following his own interpretation, provided that it is based on sound reasoning, and not on impulse merely ; and that the conception does not materially interfere with the composer's special indications.   Far from being a liberty taken with the composition, hardly enough of importance can be attached to the discovery and the bringing out of hidden melodic strains.   Far better, to give prominence to those little melodic touches, though the composer does not indicate them, than to pass them over unrecognized.

SHORT THEMES AND MOTIVES.

In those parts of a composition which lack a leading or fully developed melody, the principal theme, or even the mere motive of that theme, should be treated with the same dynamic consideration, i. e., receiving primary power, as though either theme or motive were an entire melody.

For example, in Beethoven's Sonata, Op. 53, the chief theme of the last movement is this :

or, rhythmically merely, thus :

This theme occurs in several harmonic garbs during the movement; of course, always as the primary idea. But, even when the mere motive of it appears, ♪ 𝄾 ♩ | ♩ , no matter how often, or how disguised, the motive should always receive a dynamic importance equal to that of the entire theme; thus:

In this illustration and the succeeding sixty-two measures, the figure, ♪ 𝄾 ♩ | 𝅗𝅥 , is to be treated as if it were the leading melody (which, in fact, it is), and should in every case have precedence in power over all other matter. Also here:

The motive, ♪ 𝄾 ♩ | 𝅗𝅥 , has always primary power.

I can, of course, merely hint at these matters, as to explain them fully would require oral communication. However, all that has been said in reference to the dynamic rank of themes and motives, will bear application to any sonata or other piece of music; the main point being, that any part of a leading theme claims primary dynamic power over its surroundings, the same as an entire leading melody would do.

SEVERAL MELODIES COMING TOGETHER.

This occurs in two ways; either the melodies are of equal dynamic importance, or one voice is the principal, the other (or others) being secondary.

1. Several Melodies of Equal Importance.

This happens more particularly in duos, trios, etc., written or arranged for the pianoforte, but may happen temporarily in any composition. Examples are not necessary. One word of advice, however, may be given.

If the melodies are really played with equal power of touch, the upper one, by reason of its higher pitch, will naturally be the more acute, and thus predominate. To avoid this, and in order to properly balance the melodies, the lower one can well bear, and even ought to receive, so much greater emphasis as will cause the perfect blending of both voices, so that neither of them shall predominate.

2. Several Melodies of Unequal Importance.

A good example of these is the following:

CHOPIN—POLONAISE, Op. 26, No. 1.

Also this :

CHOPIN—BALLADE, Op. 23.

The dynamic power, which is required on each of these melodies, is, of course, regulated by the relative importance which is assigned to them. One of the melodies being considered the principal, the other is naturally its counterpoint, or second in importance ; hence, second in power.

Now, it happens frequently that the counterpoint, when of a brilliant and ornamented character, is, so to speak, made too much of, to the detriment of the melody or *cantus firmus*.

Therefore great care must be taken, that the chief melody is not smothered by its brilliant or ornamental surroundings (whether appearing as counterpoint or as variation) ; for example :

WEBER—Sonata in C, Op. 24.

HENSELT—Variations de Concert, Op. 1. Var. 3.

BEETHOVEN—Sonata, Op. 53.

The importance of deciding positively which of two simultaneous melodies is the principal one can hardly be overrated; and the necessity of bringing this perception clearly before the listener, must be evident to every one. And yet, this A-B-C of dynamics is more often neglected than attended to, the secondary melody (particularly, when in the treble) being allowed to come out as if it were the principal one, while the latter (especially, when in an inner voice) is kept in the background.

The last example from Beethoven's Sonata, Op. 53, furnishes an instance of such intentional or unintentional mal-interpretation; most pianists, even those of high standing, giving to the counterpoint in the treble the chief significance, and leaving to the *cantus firmus* in the left hand either a secondary rank, or no significance at all.

This proves again that intelligent perception should precede and direct the mechanical execution.

INCIDENTAL MELODIES.

These are imperfectly developed melodies, little melodic snatches, or short phrases, occurring incidentally as the second to a primary melody. Though generally plainly perceptible, they are not unfrequently hidden in the inner voices or accompaniment, and thus are not always recognized; for example:

CHOPIN—NOCTURNE, Op. 55, No. 1.

The secondary melody is here plainly discernible.

CHOPIN—ETUDE, Op. 25, No. 1 (Sixteenth Measure).

And here, it is completely hidden, perhaps not even premeditated by the composer.

The bringing-out of hidden melodies, or even of mere fragments of them, is always permissible, though the composer may not have intended them. It would be absurd to say this is not allowed, for that would negative individuality, and confine interpretation to straight lines merely. Exactly because such fragments have not been indicated, the bringing-out of them, where they were not expected, gives evidence of artistic intelligence, and is sure to denote, on the part of the interpreter, a certain refinement of thought which cannot fail to be appreciated.

We ought not to blame a composer, for having omitted to indicate these intentional or unintentional inner thoughts. We might as well reproach a poet for not explaining every passage in his writings.

THE DYNAMICS OF FUNDAMENTAL BASSES.

The power of fundamental basses is only slightly inferior to that of the chief melody, and is equal, if not superior, to that of secondary melody or counterpoints.

On account of their inferior penetrating power, compared to treble notes, fundamental basses can bear a slight excess of power, without fear of overshadowing melodic notes in a higher register.

The additional emphasis given to fundamental basses would also be justified, on account of grammatical and quantitative principles.

Schumann's saying: "*An den Bässen erkennt man den Musiker*" ("by the basses one recognizes the musician"), which he intended in reference to composers only, might be applied with equal truth to pianists. Many of these, if put to the test upon this maxim, would fall grievously short in what is to be expected from a musician, viz., that the basses should be distinctly heard.

Fundamental basses must, naturally, either remain stationary, or move. The former we call "organ-points," the latter "progressive basses."

Progressive basses generally constitute melodic phrases, and these should receive the prominence which is due to melodies. As these phrases occur entirely in the extreme lower voice, they require even more stress than secondary melodies. In fact, if the stress were as great as that given to the chief melody, the power would not be too excessive; for example:

BEETHOVEN—Sonata, Op. 2, No. 2.

Bass Melody.

ete.

CRAMER—Etude (Bülow Edition), No. 7.

Bass Melody.

ten.

There are also cases in which the fundamental basses positively require the greatest dynamic power. This occurs—

a. When the basses constitute a continuous melody, which takes the part of second to an upper voice, as in a duet between a bass and higher voice; for example:

PRUDENT—Lucia.

The greater stress given here to the bass melody has not the object of overshadowing the upper voice, but of balancing with it, so that both can be plainly distinguished as separate voices.

b. The basses may also have primary power, when the chief melody is not a singing one, but an ornamented, running melody, as in the following etude; for example:

CHOPIN—ETUDE, Op. 25, No. 2.

The Basses having Primary Power.

Klindworth (in his revised edition of Chopin) is quite right in connecting these bass notes, by giving to each the value of an entire measure. This altered notation is both logical and in confirmation of general practice.

c. Or, when the progression of the basses represents an independent motive; as, for example:

BEETHOVEN—SONATA APPASSIONATA, Op. 57.

16

There are also other instances in which the fundamental basses demand special prominence; but, as these can neither be enumerated nor classified, the only guidance for determining their dynamic power must be their melodic importance, always remembering that any melody in the extreme bass can bear stronger stress than melodies occurring in a higher register.

THE DYNAMICS OF ACCOMPANIMENTS.

These I may dismiss with a simple word of warning.

Accompaniments have no dynamic rank at all, excepting a negative one, that of being least important.

Although this maxim is a very simple one, still it is often forgotten, and more faults are made in playing the accompaniment too loudly, than in playing the melody too softly.

This warning is particularly to be remembered during periods of an increasing intensity, or *crescendo*, because there is always the danger to be guarded against, of increasing the power of the accompaniment beyond its tertiary degree, and thus making it too prominent.

Professor Wenzel, of the Leipzig Conservatory, used to repeat over and over again to his pupils, " Do not put the expression into the accompaniment!"

Let the student follow old Wenzel's advice, and always keep the accompaniment in its proper dynamic rank.

CHAPTER XIV.

CRESCENDO AND DIMINUENDO.

AS the different degrees of tone-power give to a composition the needed dynamic colors, and accents the finishing touches, so do *crescendo* and *diminuendo* represent the gradations in the coloring, and sudden dynamic changes the contrasts of light and shade.

Crescendo is an increase of power or intensity, the result of a pressure of emotion (not of motion, for that is *accelerando*).

Diminuendo is the reverse.

Crescendo, in its climax, reaches the height of excitement or tone-power, and *diminuendo* attains perfect repose or softness.

Not only does *crescendo* commence on a softer, and end on a louder tone, but it begins on a lower and ends on a higher one.

Diminuendo being the opposite.

This is simply a matter of fact, which has its parallel in every-day life.

I remember a little scene at a European fish-market. One of the fish-wives said something which displeased another one. A quarrel ensued. Immediately a *crescendo* of both their voices commenced, not only by an increase of lung power, but by a simultaneous rising in pitch of the voice, until, at the climax, the loudest as well as highest screaming was attained.

At that moment, a well-dressed customer approached; and, as business was evidently paramount to passion, the women instantly calmed down. The voices fell in a surprisingly short *diminuendo* both in pitch and power, and the height of *crescendo* was succeeded by a sudden lull.

Here, then, we have, not an instance, but a natural law, which is instinctively followed by humanity, and, when transferred to music, gives us the fundamental rule :

Every melody or passage ascending demands a crescendo; and every melody or passage descending demands a diminuendo.

According to this rule, every *crescendo* in a rising motion, or *diminuendo* in a falling motion, is normal, regular, positive.

And every *crescendo* in a falling motion, or *diminuendo* in a rising motion, is abnormal, irregular, negative.

In other words: the former make the rule, the latter are exceptions.

Other kinds of *crescendos* and *diminuendos,* yet to be explained, are neither normal nor abnormal, and may be designated as neutral, and counted among the exceptions.

These exceptions, however, have quite as much right of existence as the rule itself, and, like other negative matters in music, are not only necessary as contrasts, but particularly needed in many instances, where normal *crescendos* or *diminuendos* would be out of place.

To point out these instances, I begin by classifying *crescendo* and *diminuendo* into the following four kinds:

1. NORMAL KIND—*Crescendo* in rising, or *diminuendo* in falling motion.

2. NEUTRAL KIND—*Crescendo* and *diminuendo* in neutral motion, *i. e.,* motion which neither rises nor falls.

3. NEUTRAL KIND—*Crescendo* toward, and *diminuendo* from, an accented point.

4. ABNORMAL KIND—*Crescendo* in falling, or *diminuendo* in rising motion.

Each of these four kinds will be reviewed in the order here indicated.

I. Crescendo in Rising—Diminuendo in Falling Motion.
(*Normal.*)

This kind is so easily understood, and so self-suggestive, that it is almost superfluous to illustrate it. The extreme upper note in any group or phrase is the terminating note of the *crescendo,* and, in returning, the initial one of the *diminuendo;* for example:

When this is not the case, the dynamic gradation is not normal.

I subjoin, however, one other example which will, likewise, re-illustrate the rhythmical arrangement of a cadence, which by the composer was left to the tender mercies of *ad libitum* interpretation (see page 60).

BEETHOVEN—Sonata, Op. 31, No. 1, in G-Major.

Altered Notation.

The interpretation of this cadence demanded, before all, a comprehensible rhythmical arrangement. The latter prepared the way for proper phrasing; and, through the phrasing, the melodic outlines of the cadence were thrown into relief. The *crescendo* and *diminuendo* suggested by the ascent and descent of the arranged movement were thus easily and accurately located, which could not have been done without previous phrasing; nor the phrasing, without previous rhythmical arrangement.

(The student is advised to compare the original notation of this cadence with the altered version.)

2. Crescendo and Diminuendo in Neutral Motion.
(*Neutral.*)

Any motion which does not actually ascend or descend, but continues spinning around in about the same tone-circle, requires swelling and decreasing, to give it color and variety; for example:

A *trill*,

which would be very tame without such dynamic accent.

Or, a *tremolo* like this:

MOZART—Fᴀɴᴛᴀsɪᴀ.

Or, a note several times repeated:

CHOPIN—Lᴀ ᴄɪ ᴅᴀʀᴇᴍ, Op. 2

CHOPIN—Nᴏᴄᴛᴜʀɴᴇ, E-Flat.

CHOPIN—Scherzo (B-Flat Minor).

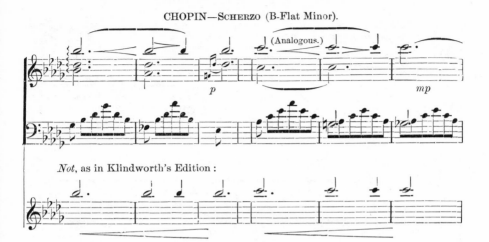

Not, as in Klindworth's Edition :

Or, a rolling, spinning-around motion :

CHOPIN—Valse, Op. 64.

CHOPIN—Nocturne (E-Flat).

SCHUBERT—Clavierstück.

BEETHOVEN—Sonata, Op. 7.

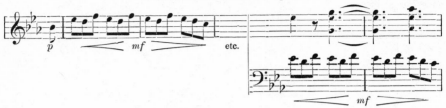

BEETHOVEN—Sonata Pathetique.

to which the following ground-bass is analogous :

Such rolling motion may be met with in almost any composition.

Although every one of such instances demands dynamic coloring, yet not every instance calls for the same kind of coloring.

Dynamic gradation, as we know, consists of either

Crescendo, ————, or

Diminuendo, ————, or

Both combined, ————, *i. e.*, the *Swell*.

Thus, we have three ways of coloring.

Now, let it be noted, that *any neutral motion which does not start from, or move toward, an accented point, has its climax (or swell) in the centre of the motion.* (See the given examples.)

But, if the motion has its climax, *i. e.*, its greatest stress, at the beginning, *sf* ⟹; or at the end, ⟸ *sf*, then there must be no swelling in the centre.

This brings us to the third kind of dynamic gradations.

3. Crescendo going toward, Diminuendo starting from, an Accented Point. (*Neutral.*)

MOZART—FANTASIA.

MENDELSSOHN—RONDO CAPRICCIOSO.

MENDELSSOHN—SPINNING-SONG.

In these illustrations, *crescendo* only was needed. In the following, both *crescendo* and *diminuendo* are required.

BEETHOVEN—Sonata, Op. 7, E-Flat (Breitkopf & Härtel Edition).

I have not added any *cresc.* or *dimin.* signs, in order to give the exact notation of Beethoven, according to the latest Breitkopf and Härtel edition.

This example is also another instance of " hidden melody," which, as a first consideration, should be brought out with unmistakable clearness.

The harmonic foundation is broken into triplets. These triplets bring animation and vigor into the movement, as the *crescendos* and *diminuendos* give dynamic coloring to the melody. But, to give this coloring intelligently, the melody pure and simple must first be precisely fixed.

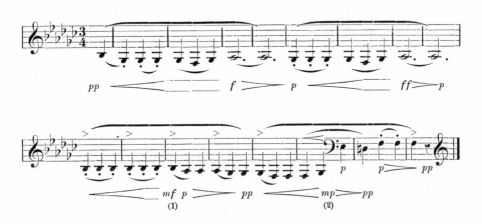

(1) = Sudden change.   (2) *mp* = *mezzopiano*, a degree between *piano* and *mezzoforte*.

Then only can dynamic gradation be accurately located.

The principle of increasing the stress toward, and decreasing it from an accented point, is applicable to the shortest groups or phrases as well as to extended ones; for example:

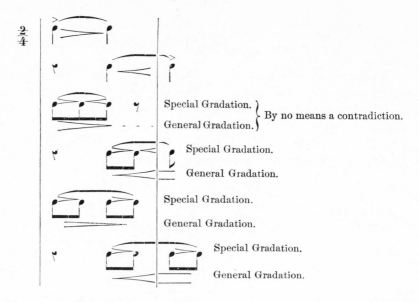

These examples show that *special* gradations may be within a *general crescendo* or *diminuendo*. By means of such "wheels within a wheel," the player is enabled to render tonic repetitions, or sequences, each time in a dynamically different measure; for example:

MOZART—SONATA IN B-FLAT.

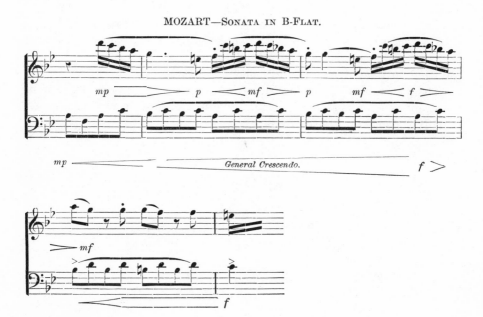

Observe the variety in the special grading, while the general tendency of *crescendo* is kept up.

MOZART—SAME SONATA.

General Crescendo.

BEETHOVEN—SONATA, Op. 31 (in E-Flat).

General Crescendo.

4. Crescendo in falling, Diminuendo in rising Motion.
(*Abnormal.*)

This kind of gradation, though theoretically abnormal, is still quite logical.

When the higher extreme of a downward motion is stronger than the terminating extreme below, of course the downward gradation is a *diminuendo*, and normal. But if the higher point is the weaker, the lower extreme the stronger, the downward motion is then, logically, a *crescendo*.

And, likewise, if a rising motion begins with the strongest stress, the rising movement dying away, then the upward gradation is properly a *diminuendo*.

It is, therefore, the relative power of the two extreme points, which determines the mode of gradation.

A few examples may complete the explanation:

Ascending Diminuendo.

CHOPIN—Valse, Op. 64, No. 2.

BEETHOVEN—Kreutzer Sonata.

Descending Crescendo.

CHOPIN—Valse, Op. 64, No. 1.

WEBER—Sonata in D-Minor.

CHOPIN—Impromptu, Op. 29.

SUDDEN DYNAMIC CHANGES.

The object of such changes is evidently contrast; and the composer's intention, in this respect, is in almost all cases plainly indicated.

Looking upon the effect of such contrasts from the point of good taste, and judging them by their appropriateness and beauty, we find that any sudden *forte* after *piano* is never beautiful or appropriate, unless it comes at the beginning of a phrase.

For instance, a phrase having terminated *p* or *pp*, a new one may begin *forte ;* whereas, if a sudden *forte* occurred within a *piano* phrase, the effect would be like that of a sudden slap in the face.

On the other hand, a sudden *piano* after a *forte* may happen anywhere, at any moment, without being offensive; for example:

BEETHOVEN—Sonata, Op. 27, No. 1 (in E-Flat Major).

Reverse here the dynamic contrast, and mark how ugly the effect would be.

Therefore, a sudden *forte* immediately after *piano* (if at all) should be given very reservedly, and in full consciousness of its fitness.

This principle coincides with the warning given with regard to exaggerated accentuation.

In fact, the following may be safely laid down as a general principle:

Piano after forte, = fp, is never offensive, and usually of good effect.

Forte after piano, = pf, is almost always objectionable, and generally incorrect.

As a proof, if proof is needed, the sign *pf* never occurs, while the sign *fp* is frequently met with.

It may be taken for granted, that a sudden *forte* following a *diminuendo,* ——— *f,* is in very questionable taste, and should be avoided, as either the *diminuendo* or the *forte* is surely incorrect.

For this reason, the following example from

BEETHOVEN—Sonata, Op. 28.

should have this descending *crescendo,*

although the *crescendo* is not indicated in the original notation.

The opposite, however, a sudden *piano* following a *cresc.,*  *p,* is frequently of beautiful effect. Notably the older masters—Haydn, Mozart, and Beethoven—were quite in the habit of employing the dynamic effect; for example:

MOZART—Sonata in A.

BEETHOVEN—Sonata, Op. 28.

sempre staccato.

BEETHOVEN—Sonata, Op. 31 (in E-Flat).

In every one of such instances, however, a slight break, or breath-taking (,) is needed between the final *crescendo* and the succeeding *piano*. This is to be effected by hand-raising and a very short rest,  *p.*

The same punctuation is needed when similar instances occur in modern compositions ; for example :

CHOPIN—Polonaise, Op. 53.

CHOPIN—Nocturne, Op. 55, No. 1.

HENSELT—Etude, Op. 2, No. 2.

17

In cases, where little groups or short phrases occur over again, it is frequently an appropriate contrast to repeat the group or phrase *piano* or *pianissimo*, in the manner of an echo. When this mode of contrast is so conceived and, after due reflection, decided upon, the interpreter is then quite justified in carrying out his conception, although the composer may not have given such indication; for example:

See illustration of Beethoven's cadence (page 245); also the following:

MOZART—Sonata in A. *Alla Turca.*

HÄNDEL—The Harmonious Blacksmith.

PART VI.

TIME.

THE term, " time," is used, musically, in a threefold sense.

In a general sense, it signifies *rhythm ;* in particular, it means *tact* and *tempo.*

Rhythm does not here require any further explanation.

We have, therefore, only to do with the two latter meanings.

CHAPTER XV.

TACT AND TEMPO.

TACT has been generalized as " a particular rhythm, exclusively adapted to music," but would be better explained as " a specific rhythm within a definite tempo." Still more closely defined, tact is that prescribed portion of a musical rhythm within a definite tempo, which serves as standard of measurement for the whole movement.

I need not go into explanatory details. These would be a repetition only of what has already been said on the subject, under " Rhythm and Metric." But I would remark that tact is the smaller measure of time, within the larger measure of tempo, and is of greater consequence than tempo. D. G. Türk (Klavierschule, 1789) says in reference to execution : " Tact-keeping is more important than velocity ; " and Moscheles (Studies, Op. 70) declares, " Tact is the soul of music."

To keep tact means :

Elementary—To give to each note its proper duration (really, a rhythmical matter).

Then—To play the notes in obedience to a regular beat, making the beat the master, the notes (*i. e.*, fingers) the servant.

And finally—To beat in accordance with a definite rate of speed.

It is universally conceded, that tact-keeping is the chief and most imperative requirement of every musical performance, more essential even than playing the notes correctly.

Far better to sacrifice a handful of notes than to stammer; but, still better, to modify the tempo by taking it slower and playing the notes correctly, than to keep up the tempo and sacrifice clearness.

Thus we may conclude, that tact-keeping is more indispensable than either clearness or tempo, and clearness more essential than tempo.

Hence, the order would be:

First, tact; then, clearness; and last, tempo.

Tact-keeping is so elementary a condition, that, as a matter of course, any one aiming at expression is supposed to be a perfect master of it.

Strict time-keeping involves naturally strict adherence to a chosen tempo; though it does not imply that the tempo is the correct one. Thus, several musicians may play the same piece in perfect time, yet, each one in a different tempo, and neither in the composer's intended one.

On the other hand, playing out of time (now faster, now slower) involves playing out of tempo.

But there is this difference:

The tempo may be intentionally hastened or slackened by a master; or, the steady time-keeping may be unintentionally interrupted by a bungler.

Out-of-time playing may, thus, be either an allowable liberty, or an inexcusable fault.

Tact, as everything else in music, has its positive and negative side: uninterrupted, perfect time being the positive; occasional, imperfect time, the negative.

The former is called in German: " Taktfestigkeit " or " tact-strictness; the latter, " Taktfreiheit " or " tact-freedom."

Now, as much as tact-strictness is indispensable to a musician, so is tact-freedom essential to the artist.

Dr. Marx says, " Tact-freedom, not strictness, is a law of nature, and based on the wave-like pulsion of the emotions."

But freedom must not be confounded with license, carelessness, or remissness. On the contrary, the fact should never be lost sight of, that absolute strictness, machine-like perfection in time-keeping, is not artistic.

Taking it as granted, that the student is " taktfest," *i. e.*, capable of keeping strict time, I take up the question of tact and tempo from its negative (or artistic) side—that of *freedom with underlying strictness.*

Tact-freedom implies the faculty of hastening or slackening the tempo, knowingly and intentionally, at such temporary moments as the character of the movement not only suggests and justifies, but even requires. To which must be added the ableness and certainty of returning to the normal tempo, whenever needed.

This shows expertness and masterly control.

On the other hand, *out-of-time playing* implies the weakness of hastening the tempo, unknowingly and unintentionally, at any random moment. To which may be added the danger of running away, and the certainty of not returning to the normal degree.

This proves inexpertness and bungling incapacity.

TEMPO.

Tempo imparts the degree of rapidity with which a piece is to be executed, and also the adherence to that degree.

In the latter meaning, tempo is synonymous with time-keeping (or tact), while in the former significance it is independent.

In this independent sense, tempo has five fundamental degrees (analogous to dynamics).

1. Very Slow............... *Largo*, etc.
2. Slow..................... *Adagio*, etc.
3. Moderate................ *Andante*, etc.
4. Fast.................... *Allegro*, etc.
5. Very Fast............... *Presto*, etc.

Each of these degrees is usually indicated, at the beginning of a movement, by some conventional Italian word or words.

These refer, however, more to the general character of the movement than to the absolute degree of rapidity ; for example:

" *Andante cantabile*," " *Allegretto grazioso*," " *Allegro con brio*," etc.

Without going into any details of this supposed well-known musical terminology, I pass on to the more exact method of indicating the composer's intention as to tempo, viz., to the beat of the metronome.

The test of a metronome is that, when set at 60, it shall beat seconds ; the unit of the beats, whatever their number may be, being always a minute.

Thus, "M. M. $\quad$ = 112" signifies that 112 beats of the metronome, each representing a quarter-note ($\quad$), are to fill up the space of a minute.

In principle, the metronome is, mathematically and astronomically, as correct as any good clock is supposed to be.

The unit being always a minute.

A minute being the 60th part of an hour.

An hour, the 24th part of a day.

A day, the 365th part of a year.

And a year, the time it takes the earth to go around the sun.

Here we have a positive standard of measurement, which it has as yet been impossible to discover for measuring the degrees of dynamics.

In practice, however, a metronome is seldom as correct as a good clock, but that is not necessary.

Our slowest time is said to be forty quarter-notes in a minute; our fastest, two hundred and eight quarter-notes in a minute. And this corresponds to the figures on the dial of a metronome, which begin at 40, and end at 208.

The choice of tempo is a matter of great moment, and should be decided upon more in accordance with the intrinsic character of the composition, than extrinsic effect; particularly, as a mistaken tempo will injure a performance more, than a well-chosen tempo, alone, could benefit it.

Subjectiveness and objectiveness—as the Germans are fond of saying—play a great role in the choice of tempo, and, frequently, even a greater one than the composer's positive indication.

Now, as a rule, these indications should be obeyed; and only where there is any reasonable doubt as to their genuineness should the interpreter consider himself justified in substituting his own tempo, unless he means to place his judgment above that of the composer.

It is a strange thing, that errors, in respect to tempo, like errors in dynamics, are more frequently committed in the direction of going too far, than of going not far enough.

In dynamic, far more faults are committed in playing too loudly, than in playing too softly; and, in tempo, far more mistakes occur in playing too quickly, than in playing too slowly.

Such tempo-faults are not only committed by immature piano-players, who hurry mostly from nervousness, but also by technically-finished players; more particularly, the virtuosos, who wish thus to display their technique in a more brilliant light.

The true artist does not go beyond the limit where beauty ceases and pyrotechnics begin; while the mere virtuoso, catering for the public, unfortunately prefers pyrotechnics.

Although it is not in my, or any person's, power to lay down a rule with regard to the choice of tempo, I may give a general warning against overdoing, by advising the careful player never to take any tempo too fast, but always a little slower than his technique is able to execute. There should always be a margin left for eventualities, such as nervousness, indisposition, fatigue, etc. This margin should be employed in paying attention to other matters beside velocity, such as listening to one's self, and improving the execution through an always discriminating touch and ever-watchful intelligence.

At all events, the fact is not to be disputed, that, only when the performer's powers are far beyond the piece, can he expect to play it faultlessly.

Playing should not be laboring, but playing, in the literal meaning of the word.

If the performer can impress the listener with a feeling of confidence and ease, he will probably succeed in giving pleasure; but the moment he awakens a feeling of uneasiness in his audience, the chances of success are hopeless.

Therefore, moderation in tempo, like moderation in dynamics, should be the ruling principle. Repose and self-command should always hold in control the mechanical portion of the performance. Even in the fastest *prestissimo*, or in the most passionate *abandon*, the mind must be the master, the fingers only servants.

Tact-freedom comprises all those transgressions and infringements of strict time, including tempo, which are deliberately resorted to for the purpose of imparting artistic variety to the stiffness of unchanging measured motion.

Such permissible transgressions I enumerate as follows:

1. ACCELERANDO.	3. SUDDEN TEMPO CHANGES.
2. RITARDANDO.	4. TENUTO AND FERMATA.

5. RUBATO.

Each of these we shall now successively investigate.

CHAPTER XVI.

ACCELERANDO AND RITARDANDO.

I PURPOSE treating these subjects in an entirely different manner from that hitherto pursued in this work, viz.: by citing what others have said about them, and merely adding a few glossaries.

The few writers who, to my knowledge, have written to any purpose on the application of *accelerando* and *ritardando* are:

1. C. CZERNY, in his "Pianoforteschule," Op. 500, Third Part.
2. DR. AD. KULLAK, in "Die Aesthetik des Clavierspiels."
3. MATH. LUSSY, in his "Traité de l'expression musicale."

Let us begin with Czerny.

———

CZERNY, who, on account of the almost incredible number of his velocity exercises, is frequently styled "the Man of Velocity" (der Mann der Geläufigkeit), was also, undoubtedly, both in his musical and theoretical works, "der Mann der Praxis," viz.: the practical.

The theoretical portion of his great "Pianoforte-School," notably, its Third Part, which treats "Von dem Vortrag," was not only, at the time of its appearance, the first and foremost literary work on the subject of interpretation, style, and expression (Vortrag), but remains to the present day one of the most notable and complete treatises on those subjects.

Notwithstanding Czerny's manner of treatment being now generally considered somewhat superficial, we have nothing clearer or more practical. He is, beyond all, too little of an idealist, and too much of a realist, ever under the mantle of vague phrases to attempt going beyond his own or his reader's depth. And, though he rarely enters into close details or explanations, yet, as an old practitioner (Practicus), he has the good sense to go straight to his point.

The third chapter of the Third Part is entitled, "Von den Veränderungen des Zeitmasses;" more particularly, "about the uses of *accelerando* and *ritardando*."

After some preliminary observations, in which he says:—"Not only every composition, but every part of a composition, expresses some definite emotion," (?) " or " (as he prudently adds), " at least, permits such emotion to be subjoined by the interpreter or through the interpretation," he mentions a number of emotions which require a *ritardando*, and others, an *accelerando*. Going then from the inner purport of a composition to its outer structure, from the æsthetical to the material part of his subject, or from the spiritual to the tangible, he feels at once more at home, and becomes precise and clear. He begins:

" Many, in fact, nearly every place or point in a composition, which is susceptible of tact-freedom, can bear more than one mode of employing *rallentandos* and *accelerandos*, without any one of these modes being absolutely faulty or inappropriate. So, for example, can the following little melody be interpreted in four different ways: "

CZERNY—ANDANTE.

FOUR DIFFERENT WAYS OF INTERPRETATION.

1. In *tempo*	throughout.	
2. In *tempo*	*un poco ritenuto*	*smorzando.*
3. In *tempo*	*poco accelerando*	*rallentando.*
4. In *tempo.*	*molto ritardando*	*perdendosi.*

Then he asks:

" Which of these four kinds of interpretation may now be the best ? "

Leaving this an open question, he gives the good advice:

" When any musical idea, any group, or phrase, or passage, recurs in various places of a composition, then the performer is not only at liberty, but it should be his duty, to alter the mode of rendering at each repetition, in order to avoid monotony. But, in deciding upon this variation, he has to consider what precedes and what follows, and then determine his mode of rendering accordingly.

" *Ritardando* is, as a rule, far more generally applicable than *accelerando*, because it does not impair the character of a piece as much as a too frequently recurring *accelerando.* would do."

In reference to the employment of *accelerando*, Czerny gives no rule at all, mentioning only that "*accelerando* is used in ascending movements, and announces passion and agitation;" but, regarding *ritardando*, he is more diffuse, giving the following rules:

"Ritardando is most appropriately employed—

"RULE 1.—Before the return of a principal theme.

"RULE 2.—On those notes within a period which lead to the beginning of a phrase or even a mere section.

"RULE 3.—On accented long notes, followed by shorter ones.

"RULE 4.—Before going over into a different tact, *i. e.*, just before the change of time begins.

"RULE 5.—Immediately before a pause or rest.

"RULE 6.—On the *diminuendo* of a part which was just before very lively, as also on brilliant passages, when suddenly a run occurs which requires a soft and delicate rendering.

"RULE 7.—On all embellishments of many quick notes, which one finds it difficult to get comfortably into the strict measure of time.

"RULE 8.—Occasionally, also, on the ascending *crescendo* of an especially emphasized part, leading to an important climax or to an ending.

"RULE 9.—On very humorous, capricious, or fantastic parts or passages, to elevate their character.

"RULE 10.—Almost wherever the composer has marked '*espressivo*,' and

"RULE 11.—At the end of every long trill, as on every soft cadence in general.

"As a matter of course, all that is said with regard to *ritardando* refers equally to such synonymous words as '*rallentando, ritenuto, smorzando, calando*,' etc."

Here he gives the following example, with his annexed remarks:

1st Measure.—Strictly in tempo.

2d Measure.—The last three eighths are to be almost imperceptibly retarded ; because the next measure brings a repetition of the first, or chief, motive (Rule 2).

3d Measure.—The last arpeggio-chord should be slightly retarded.

4th Measure.—The last three eighths should be played with a little more warmth (almost *accelerando*), which diminishes in the next measure only.

5th Measure.—The embellishment, according to Rule 7, a little *ritardando*.

6th Measure.—A *ritard.* on this kind of embellishment is always permissible—even necessary—as a preventive of an awkward or hasty rendering, and an assistance in performing the quick notes in a delicate, graceful manner, as though the notes were gradually vanishing.

Toward the end of the embellishment only, should the *ritard.* become perceptible, and a slight pause should be made on the G-sharp, the last note but one.

7th and 8th Measures.—Strictly in time.

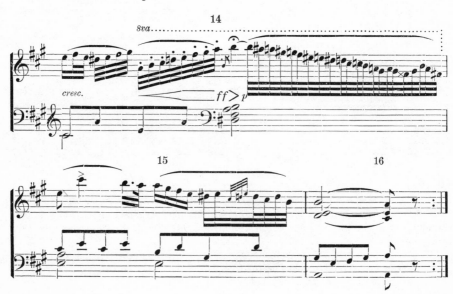

9th Measure.—With warmth and strength ; consequently, almost *accelerando.*

10th Measure.—The second half of this measure, more quickly.

11th Measure.—A little *ritardando*, and the last dissonant chord very softly ; because every dissonating chord (when *piano*) is more effective if played in this way.

12th Measure.—The first three eighths in tempo, but the last five eighths decidedly *ritardando*, inasmuch as they lead to the theme (Rule 1).

13th Measure.—In tempo.

14th Measure.—The first quarter is already rather *ritard.*, which increases considerably in the second quarter ; while the eight upper notes should be strongly marked, and *crescendo.* The fermate, ⌢, lasts about three eighths, and the subsequent run is moderately fast, delicate, and *diminuendo,* until the last eight notes become quite prominently *ritardando.*

15th Measure.—The first half is in tempo, the second half *ritardando,* while the end of the embellishment should softly die away. The *ritardando* is here most necessary, as the measure contains the soft and tender finale cadence.

Last Measure.—Quietly, in tempo.

The following observations should be well considered :

1. Although this theme has a *ritardando* in almost every measure, yet the prevailing time of the whole should never be vacillating or unsteady (especially in the accompanying left hand), so that the listener is never in any doubt about the proper time.

2. As every part is to be performed twice, so, the second time, each mode of rendering, consequently, every *ritardando,* may be given more prominently, whereby the whole gains in interest.

"Rule 12.—Every sudden modulation, or change of key, should be made apparent, by a change of tempo also ; for example :

The first five measures, in tempo.

In the *6th Measure,* gradually *ritardando.*

In the *7th Measure,* a quieter movement, which must not, however, depart too much from the prescribed general tempo.

In the *8th Measure,* gradual return to the first tempo.

N.B.—Although the first two measures in this example are repeated, it would not be well to render them the second time *piano,* because these measures are succeeded by another *piano.*

The reader will perceive by this, that every rule of expression depends on minor circumstances.

"Rule 13.—If the new key is to be rendered *forte,* and the modulation to it *piano,* then the new key should enter in tempo, or even a little *accelerando;* for example:

"Rule 14.—When the transition into a theme is composed of *staccato* notes or chords, a *ritardando* would be quite appropriate toward the end; but, when the transition is composed of rapid or *legato* notes, then a strict tempo, or, according to circumstances, even an *accelerando* would be more suitable; for example:

SECOND EXAMPLE.

The *ritardando*, in the first example, might also be given in a very prominent degree (*molto ritard.*), and with a great deal of humor, if the character of the whole permit such mode of expression.

DR. A. KULLAK, ON ACCELERANDO AND RITARDANDO.

Dr. AD. KULLAK (brother of Theodore, the celebrated pianist,) is as hyper-æsthetical, as Czerny is essentially practical.

His last and best literary works, "Das musikalisch Schöne, Beitrag zur Æsthetik der Tonkunst," (Leipzig, 1858,) and "Die Æsthetik des Klavierspiels," (Berlin, 1861,) contain, according to the critic in Mendel's Mus. Conv.-Lex., "beside a great deal that is far-fetched, much that is worthy of notice." In his "Æsthetik des Klavierspiels," Dr. Kullak makes the same mistake which so many others have made, viz., he treats musical interpretation, expression, etc., too much from an idealistic, and too little from a realistic side. (The reverse of Czerny.)

He burdens and obscures his statements with perpetual and hindering reflections on feeling and mood, and cannot get over the (for once and all) unanalyzable, unteachable portion of his subject—the emotions. His idealistic leanings lead him to the use of overwhelming phrases, which, though they give evidence of the author's fine æsthetical sense, are not calculated to give the reader a clear and practical explanation of his subject.

Omitting Kullak's high-flown phraseology, I give here only the main points of his observations on *rallentando* and *accelerando*.

"Either, the contents of a piece express certain emotions, which demand a *rallentando* or *accelerando;* or, the outer structure of the composition renders such tact-transgression necessary."

"In general, a unity or steadiness of time should prevail."

"And yet, special time-transgressions are of essential moment to musical beauty; notably, the *rallentando* is of such expressive significance, that it is rarely missing in any work."

"We proceed to the chief cases in which a *rallentando* is employed:

"1. Every note in melodic declamation, which is sufficiently significant to be emphasized, receives a *rallentando*." *

He gives here the following examples:

BEETHOVEN—Sonata, Op. 26.   Sonata, Op. 10.

MENDELSSOHN—Song without Words.

Book 1, No. 1.   Book 5, No. 1.

---

* This rule, which Dr. Kullak considers of particular importance, refers to the slight, almost imperceptible *tenuto* (*ten.* ∧) or *fermate* (⌒) on single notes, which leads so easily (especially with singers) to unsteady time-keeping, and does generally more harm than good. (See subsequent chapter, *Tenuto* and *Fermate*.)

BEETHOVEN—Sonata in D-Minor.

HUMMEL—Op. 18.

BEETHOVEN—Sonata in B-Flat, Op. 22.

"2. *Rallentando* is also there employed, where a thought terminates. Also, either at the actual ending of a piece, or at such parts of a piece which indicate an essential division." (Compare Czerny's Rules 1 and 2.) For example:

BEETHOVEN—Sonata, Op. 26.

BEETHOVEN—Sonata in D-Minor.

18

BEETHOVEN—Sonata in G-Major, Op. 14.

un poco rall.   *a tempo.*

"*Accelerando* is, in general, not so permissible as *ritardando*.

"The inner reasons which demand an *accelerando* consist in the ascent of the physical motion that is deposited in the tone-work, and in the rise of emotional activity. The outer reasons concern the charm of variety, or the brilliancy of sensuous effect.

"The ending of a thought is more fittingly depicted by *ritardando* than by *accelerando*. Yet, there are cases where an *accelerando*, at the end of a composition, is quite appropriate.

"For example, Chopin's Scherzo in B-minor (toward the end), and the finale of Beethoven's Sonata Appassionata.

"Beethoven, however, not content with a mere *accelerando*, prefers to give the closing measures as a separate (*più presto*) movement.

"A gentle *accelerando*, in this sense, suggests itself very naturally in the 'Cantilene' of Schumann's F-major Novellette:

accel.   etc.

"And in the second movement of Schumann's G-minor Sonata:

accel.

"*Accelerando* is, as a rule, appropriately employed in places where brilliancy succeeds quietness. For example, in concertos and other concert-pieces, where the passage-work commences after the 'Cantilene.'

"Also in places where unessential passages are inserted between essential themes. For example, in accompaniments, or cases like the following:

MENDELSSOHN—Præludium (E-Minor), Op. 35.

ac - ce - le - ran - do.

SCHUMANN—Sonata (G-Minor).

ac - ce - le - - - - -

First movement, the first eight measures, before the entrance of the bass-theme.

" This includes most of the brilliant cadences by Liszt, Raff, etc.

" Repetitions of a musical thought are usually rendered in a changed tempo. The first time, *accelerando;* the second, *ritardando.*

" *Accelerando* and *ritardando* are analogous to *crescendo* and *diminuendo.* An ascent in pitch, a rise of emotion, suggests naturally a *crescendo* and *accelerando* as means of expression, just as a calming-down suggests both *diminuendo* and *rallentando.*

" The union of *accelerando* with *crescendo,* and of *diminuendo* with *rallentando,* is most natural and occurs very frequently, especially in slow, expressive pieces ; for example :

BEETHOVEN—Sonata, Op. 10.

Adagio.

poco accel.

poco rallent.

" *Accelerando,* however, may go with *diminuendo,* and *ritardando* with *crescendo.*

" Brilliant passages which become softer and softer are a charm of a peculiar kind.

" The addition of a *rallentando* to a *crescendo* adds greatly to the significance of the expression ; for example :

BEETHOVEN—Sonata Pathétique.

M. LUSSY, ON ACCELERANDO AND RITARDANDO.

Here we have a writer who is very prolific on the subject.

Mathis Lussy, I presume, was still a young man when he wrote his " Traité de l'Expression Musicale," the only one of his works known to me. While carefully studying his treatise, I was favorably struck by several fine suggestions; but, as a whole, the work gives me the impression of being founded more on the casual observation of an easily impressible young teacher, jumping rather freely at conclusions, than on the deeper thoughts and learning of a mature musical scientist.

The following extract, which I give *verbatim*, represents the best of what his book contains; and his numerous examples, apart from their questionable soundness, present many curious features.

Lussy begins:

" Ascending is striving, physically as well as morally.

" It is raising one's self to a superior elevation, against the tendency of our being. The more the ascent is steep, bristling with obstacles and asperities, the more force is required, the more rapidly our pulses beat, the greater becomes our animation; but, also, the sooner we are exhausted. Once the summit being attained, we experience a certain well-being (*bien-être*); we breathe with ease—the victory makes us happy.

" This comparison furnishes us with a simple and rational explanation of the inclination, which musicians have, of hastening, at the commencement of ascending phrases, and retarding, toward the end.

" Descending, on the other hand, is reaching an inferior degree, physically as well as morally. It is following one's natural bent. And the impetus is in proportion to the length and uniformity of the descent.

" From this arises, with the musician, the inclination to accelerate, and the necessity to retard, on uniformly descending passages.

" If, in this kind of passages, the executant, following the impulse of accelerating, does not hold back the movement, he runs the risk of being precipitated with headlong velocity.

" When, however, descending groups of similar contexture occur at the end of a piece, this danger of following one's natural impulse disappears ; the impetuosity loses itself, so to say, in space, without impairing the rhythm or the movement.

" The movement, or rather, the gait of execution, is then similar to the march of a foot-traveller. As the traveller regulates his step according to the ground he passes over, so should the executant modify his movements, to conform to the structure of the composition. But, however even or uneven the surface may be, which the traveller passes over, if his course is long, fatigue will come, and paralyze his march ; and his step will become re-animated only at the appearance of the desired end, which excites all his strength, all his energies.

" From these physiological analogies ensue the following principles."

(So far the ideas are excellent, but the rules now following are far from being what Lussy considers them, viz., adequate to the purpose. But the reader may judge for himself.)

"One should Accelerate—

" 1. On several pathetic (?) notes in succession, or on a single one being exceptionally of great value, at the beginning or in the middle of a phrase.

" 2. On several similar notes or groups, having an exceptional ascending or descending progression.

" 3. On passages which present, exceptionally (in the middle of an *andante* or *adagio*), a simple contexture provoking agitation, passion.

"One should Retard—

" 1. On one or several consecutive pathetic notes, which occur so suddenly, at the beginning of a phrase, that one has neither time nor scope to make a spirited dash (*prendre élan*).

" 2. In consequence of fatigue, exhausted strength, and expended *élan*, in an ascending or descending course.

" 3. On passages which present, exceptionally (in the middle of an *allegro*), an expressive contexture, provoking calmness, gravity, sadness.

" 4. On pathetic notes and passages, on temporary repetitions, and on dissonating neighboring notes (suspensions), which occur at the end of a phrase.

"Before undertaking the application, in detail of these principles, let us make an observation of capital importance.

"The *rallentando* or *accelerando* which pathetic notes are susceptible of depends:

"*a*. On the position of notes. A note, exceptionally repeated several times, exacts at the beginning of a phrase an *accelerando*; at the end, a *rallentando*.

"*b*. On the general contexture of a piece. We have said, one hastens or slackens on passages having an *exceptional* upward or downward tendency. But, if the *general* contexture of a piece is ascending or descending, one neither retards nor hastens; for example:

AUBER—UN JOUR DE BONHEUR.

"Nevertheless, if, in a piece of ascending contexture, the motive of the first phrase is repeated in the next phrase with a more lively accompaniment than it had at first, then one should accelerate; for example:

"*c*. On the number of parts or instruments executing a composition. The soloist may permit himself modifications of the general time which the orchestra does not admit.

"*d*. On the sense of words in singing.   The tempo to verses expressing sadness, melancholy, etc., should be much slower than to those expressing joy, happiness, triumph, etc.

"OF ACCELERANDOS.

" I. *Accelerando, resulting from several pathetic notes in succession or a single one having exceptionally a great value.*

" One should Accelerate—

" 1. On a note of great value, exceptionally occurring ; for example :

MOZART—Don Giovanni.

" 2. On a note exceptionally repeated several times in succession, at the beginning or in the middle of a phrase ; for example :

MOZART—Fantasia in D-Minor.

" 3. On a group of notes exceptionally repeated, if the bass is moving either upward or downward ; for example :

BELLINI—Norma.

"But, if the bass remains stationary, there should be no *accelerando*.

"4. On upper neighboring notes (suspensions), when they are several times repeated, at the beginning of a phrase; for example:

BELLINI.

"5. On modulations, *i. e.*, during modulations; for example:

FIELD—Fifth Nocturne.

BEETHOVEN—Sonata Pathétique.

" 6. On descending groups of small valued notes, at the end of a phrase, if the note which succeeds such descending group is of larger value, or if it is followed by a suspension ; for example :

WEBER—Oberon.

CHOPIN—Mazurka, Op. 7, No. 2.

" 7. On melodic guides (guides mélodiques) of a simple, uniform con- texture and of short duration ; for example :

MOZART—Fantasia.

" II. Accelerando, resulting from similar notes and groups having an exceptional ascending or descending tendency.

"One should Accelerate—

" 8. On notes which progress exceptionally, stepwise, in an ascending movement ; for example :

HAYDN.

FIELD—Fifth Nocturne.

accel.

"9. On notes which, at the beginning of a phrase, progress exceptionally upward or downward, and having, as junction or pivot, a stationary note; for example:

WEBER—Invitation to the Dance.

"10. When, at the beginning of a phrase, the melody or bass progresses exceptionally in contrary motion, immaterial whether approaching or going apart from each other; for example:

KUHLAU—Op. 88.

accel.

"11. On similar little rhythmic groups, exceptionally repeated, in either ascending or descending motion; for example:

CHOPIN—Mazurka, Op. 6.

"12. At the end of a rapid movement, on a group of notes which are several times repeated, while the bass remains stationary; for example:

BEETHOVEN—SONATA, Op. 27, No. 2.

accel.

MOZART—MENUET FROM SONATA IN A.

accel.　　　　　　　　　　　　　　　　　　　　*rall.*

"13. On groups, or traits of similar texture, ascending or descending, at the end of periods in quick movements; for example:

MOZART—SONATA IN F.

stretto.

"III. *Accelerando, resulting from passages which present, exceptionally, a contexture provoking agitation, passion.*

"One should Accelerate—

"14. On passages containing little values, and on similar, uniform groups which have the character of playfulness in the midst of expressive phrases composed of larger valued notes; for example:

BEETHOVEN—Sonata Pathétique.

" 15. On phrases exceptionally accompanied by stationary, unbroken chords, coming after a phrase in which the chords were broken, or in which the harmonic parts pursued a steady, regular course; for example:

FIELD—Fifth Nocturne.

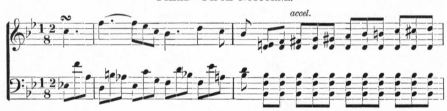

" 16. On syncopated phrases and passages, with intervening rests; for example:

MOZART—Fantasia in D-Minor.

MOZART—Sonata in F.

" 17. On exceptional phrases and passages of a syncopated contexture; for example:

BEETHOVEN—Sonata, Op. 26.

" 18. On phrases, exceptionally accompanied by ascending and descending arpeggios; for example:

MENDELSSOHN—Rondo Capriccioso, Op. 14.

più mosso.

After these rather problematical rules, Lussy goes on, with much self-satisfaction:

" Here we are only at the end of the first part of this chapter. There, where Czerny gave only one rule, we have found *eighteen*, several of which are in flagrant contradiction to his rule. Evident proof, it seems to us, that even the greatest masters have given but a cursory glance at the question.

" OF RALLENTANDO OR RITARDANDO.

" I. *Rallentando resulting, in slow or moderate movements, from one or several pathetic (?) notes, occurring consecutively at the beginning of a phrase or slurred group.*

" One should Retard—

" 19. On the rest which follows the first note of a little *staccato*-phrase, if the note is the highest of the little phrase, and is followed by a note of the same value; for example:

SCHULHOFF.

SCHULHOFF.

"20. On the initial note of a little *legato*-phrase, if it is, exceptionally, a higher note, the preceding phrases or groups having commenced with a lower note; for example:

MOZART.

"Of course, in rapid movements one should absolutely abstain from dwelling on any high initial note.

WEBER—INVITATION TO THE DANCE.

"It would be absurd to dwell on the extreme F beginning the third measure, on the pretext, that it was the highest note of the phrase. We have heard, however, this fault committed by some of our most celebrated professors.

"21. On the rest which follows the first note of a phrase, if the note is a repeated high one and arrived at by the jump of a large ascending interval, followed by a lower note; for example:

MOZART—SONATA IN F.

CHOPIN—MAZURKA, Op. 7, No. 1.

"22. On the rest which follows the highest note of an ascending course, followed by an inferior note; for example:

CHOPIN—Op. 7, No. 4.

"23. On the upper suspension of a group which, though occurring at the end of a phrase, yet belongs to the next phrase as the attacking or initial note (*note d'élan*); for example:

CHOPIN—MAZURKA, Op. 7, No. 3.

"24. On the first notes of a phrase, when the phrase commences with a sudden change of key or a character; for example:

AUBER—UN JOUR DE BONHEUR.

MOZART—FANTASIA IN D-MINOR.

"II. *Rallentando, resulting from one or more pathetic notes in the midst of a phrase.*

"One should Retard—

"25. On an exceptionally high and acute note, being the companion of a lower note; for example:

AUBER—Haydée.

"26. On the note which replaces, exceptionally, a higher or lower one, changing thus the direction of the preceding rhythmic design; for example:

MOZART—Sonata in A, Fifth Var.

"III. *Rallentando, resulting at the end of an ascent or descent, from fatigue, exhausted strength, or expended dash (élan).*

"One should Retard—

"27. At the end of an ascent or descent, especially, if the rhythmic design has just changed; for example:

CHOPIN—Op. 30, No. 2.

CHOPIN—Op. 7, No. 2.

" At the end of these examples, one retards not only on account of exhaustion, but, also, because the design of the last quarter in the finale-measures has changed its direction (see ✕).

"28. On a *suite* of ascending notes, when they are followed by a lower note in a downward jump; for example:

BEETHOVEN—Op. 49.

MOZART.

"29. On descending groups immediately following ascending ones; for example:

BELLINI—Norma.

"30. On a group of notes following high notes; for example:

MEYERBEER—Robert le Diable.

19

"IV. *Rallentando, resulting from an exceptional contexture provoking calmness, sadness, reverie, etc.*

"One should Retard—

"31. On expressive singing-passages, presenting larger valued notes and fuller harmony than before, when they occur, exceptionally, in an *allegro* composed of smaller valued notes; for example:

MOZART—Sonata in F.

"32. On expressive passages provoking reverie, interposed in the midst of a lively movement; for example:

CHOPIN—Valse, Op. 18.

"33. On passages in a minor key having previously occurred in major; for example:

BEETHOVEN—Moonlight Sonata.

MOZART—Fantasia Sonata.

" V. *Rallentando, resulting from one or several pathetic notes, at the end of a section or phrase.*

"One should Retard—

" 34. On the large valued note which occasionally precedes the finale note, especially if it has a trill; for example:

AIR ANCIEN.

" 35. On a note exceptionally repeated several times in succession; for example:

BEETHOVEN—SERENADE.

" 36. On the high note, at the end of the last but one measure, if it is syncopated, sustained, or chromatic; for example:

DONIZETTI—LUCIA.

" 37. On an upper suspension, in the last but one measure; for example:

AUBER—LA MUETTE.

CHOPIN—NOCTURNE, Op. 55, No. 1.

"38. On temporary repetitions, at the end of the last but one measure; for example:

MOZART—Fantasia.

CHOPIN—Valse.

"39. On the last but one note, if the last is a temporary repetition;
for example:

CHOPIN—Nocturne, Op. 55.

MOZART.

"40. On the repetition of a short design occurring in the last but one
measure, especially if the design contains suspensions; for example:

DONIZETTI—Lucia.

"41. On exceptional quarter-notes, in the last but one measure; for
example:

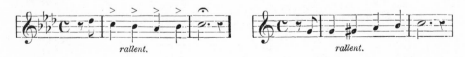

"42. On little values, occurring, exceptionally, at the end of a phrase, or in groups containing temporary repetitions or suspensions; for example:

MEYERBEER—Huguenots.

rallent.

BEETHOVEN—Moonlight Sonata.

"But, when the small values are simply ornamental notes, which together take the place of a large valued note, there should be no *ritardando*.

"43. On the last groups of notes descending, stepwise, to a *finale* note; for example:

MOZART—Don Juan.

"44. On the descending notes, at the end of the last but one measure; for example:

ROSSINI.

rallent.

"45. On the last notes preceding an incomplete ending (Germ. *Trugschluss*); for example:

SCHUBERT—Adieu.

rall.

MEYERBEER—Robert.

"46. On the end of a phrase presenting, exceptionally, several harmonic parts, resolutions of dissonances, retardations, counterpoints; for example:

WEBER—Oberon.

MERCADANTE.

"47. On the last notes of a melodic guide containing an upper suspension, a repetition, or notes turning on a pivot (*des notes pivotales*); for example:

CZERNY—Op. 139.

MOZART—Sonata in A.

"48. On organ-points, syncopes, or large values, which occur at the end of embellishments or *ad libitum* cadences; for example:

BEETHOVEN—Sonata Pathétique.

"49. On rhythmical repetitions, *i.e.*, on designs and groups of notes consecutively repeated at the end of an expressive phrase; for example:

CHOPIN—Nocturne.

CHOPIN—Mazurka.

"50. On final chords, with rests intervening; for example:

BEETHOVEN—Sonata Pathétique, Op. 13.

So far, Lussy and his rules.

Having thus quoted Lussy *verbatim*, I neither refute nor advocate his rules; because there is much in them which is good, and much which is dubious.

Perhaps, if these rules were properly sifted, curtailed, and better classified, many useful principles might be deduced from them. But, attempting, as Lussy does, to cover by a particular rule almost every instance in which either *accelerando* or *ritardando* is applicable or required, is even more problematical and hopeless, than attempting, as some grammarians do, to teach by rules the gender of French or German nouns.

The numerous and heterogeneous quotations from Czerny, Kullak, and Lussy, have, doubtless, given the reader ample material for becoming acquainted with the leading principles which govern the uses of *accelerando* and *ritardando*. And, it is hoped, the student will now be able to select from the many given rules those that are practical and generally fitting; and to take at what they are worth those that are only casually fitting, or based on personal taste.

CHAPTER XVII.

SUDDEN CHANGES OF TEMPO.

THE present subject is, really, the adjunct and complement of the previous chapter.

1. *Ritardando* or *rallentando*, etc., means: *gradual*, not *sudden* decrease of tempo, viz.: *getting* slower, not *already* slower.

Accelerando or *stringendo*, etc., means: *gradual*, not *sudden* increase of tempo, *i. e.*, *getting* faster, not *already* faster.

Both meanings are analogous to *crescendo* and *diminuendo*.

The former does not signify *forte*, but *piano*, ⤙, becoming *forte*.

The latter does not signify *piano*, but *forte*, ⤚, becoming *piano*.

It is both strange and true, that the distinction between gradation and sudden change is frequently overlooked.

Tempo has its sudden changes as well as dynamics.

A suddenly faster tempo is not an *accelerando*.

A suddenly slower tempo is not a *ritardando*.

I do not refer to those general changes of tempo which occur at the beginning of a new movement, or sometimes within a movement, but to those temporary changes within a movement which are frequently confounded with gradation, viz.: to the words,

Più—more; and *Meno*—less; and others.

These, coupled with other tempo-terms, signify an *abrupt*, not a gradual change of speed; for example:

Più mosso, Più vivo, Più allegro, Più presto, Stretto, etc.,

signify: faster, at once faster; and

Meno mosso, Più adagio, Più lento, etc.,

signify: slower, at once slower.

The difference between such a sudden change and the gradual change implied by *accelerando* and *ritardando*, etc., is frequently of great importance, and is surely worthy of careful notice.

2. The second distinction is this:

The words, *accelerando* and *ritardando*, are, strictly speaking, applicable only on a plurality of notes, and not on an individual note. To accelerate, or hasten over, an individual note, is absolutely wrong, because the rhythmical duration of the note would be curtailed and disregarded; hence, the effect would be that of bad time-keeping, instead of permissible tact-freedom.

Thus, Lussy's Rule 1 (based probably on the bad habits of singers) is certainly incorrect.

To retard an individual note or rest, although substantially permissible, is, nevertheless, a misapplication of the idea of *ritardando;* inasmuch as an individual note, or rest, may be *dwelt on*, sustained, prolonged, but cannot really be retarded, *i. e.*, become slower.

Long habit, however, has so accustomed musicians to this misapplication of the word, that very few even think of, and, still less, point out this difference which, though small, is well worth observing.

The result of accepting this difference is to bring every *ritardando* on single notes or rests (which Kullak considers of great importance, and Lussy exemplifies by a large number of illustrations) under a separate classification, viz., under the following heading:

TENUTO AND FERMATE.

The meaning of these terms implies a dwelling on, or sustaining of, a special point—a note, a chord, or rest.

But, while *tenuto* (*ten.* or ∧) is more employed within a movement, *fermate* (⌢) [French *point d'orgue, point d'arrêt;* Germ. *Ruhepunkt;* It. *corona*] is chiefly used at the end of a musical period, or cadence, and requires the longer duration of the two.

The exact duration of a *fermate* (⌢) cannot be stated, as that depends on the character and tempo of the movement. But, as general guidance, the principle may be accepted, that in slow movements a *fermate* prolongs a note about twice its value; while in a quick movement it prolongs a note at least three, even four times its value.

The fact, that *tenuto* and *fermate* refer to individual points merely, renders these terms and indications analogous, in reference to time, to what *sforzando* (*sfz, fz, rfz,* etc.,) is, in reference to dynamics. The latter referring, likewise, only to individual points.

In fact, everything connected with time has its similitude in dynamics; for example:

There are:

	IN DYNAMICS.	IN TIME.
Five Degrees............	*pp, p, m, f, ff*..............	very slow, slow, moderate, fast, very fast.
Two Gradations.........	*crescendo, diminuendo*.......	*accelerando, ritardando.*
Indications referring to Special Points.........	*forzando,* or *sf, fz, rfz, sfz,* etc.	*tenuto* = *ten. ; fermate* = ⌢.
Sudden Changes.........	*fp, ffp, fmf*..............	{ *più lento, meno mosso,* etc. { *più presto, stretto,* etc.

The analogy, in reference to individual points, is so great, and the sympathy between emphasis and duration so strong, that very frequently notes, marked *fz, sfz,* >, etc., also need a *tenuto* (*ten*). Or, in other words, emphasized points can generally bear, and frequently even demand, to be dwelt on, sustained, prolonged.

Without going into detailed examination of when and where such dwelling on or holding, viz. (*ten.*), is suitable or desirable, I simply refer the reader to

Czerny—Rules 3 and 5 ;
Kullak—Rule 1 ; and
Lussy—Rules 34 and subsequent ones ;

and also to the remarks bearing upon this subject, as given under " Accents of Extremes " (*q. v.*).

The observations and examples thus recommended are quite sufficient for the intelligent student, while it would be useless to enlighten the sleepy-minded, by entering into more explicit details.

RUBATO.

Rubato, robbed or stolen ; hence, *rubato tempo*, or *rubamento di tempo*, robbed or stolen time. The Italians have also *contra-tempo*, and the French *contre-temps*, as synonymous terms, both signifying *against the time*. It may also be observed that the simple term, *rubato*, is generally used in preference to *rubato tempo*.

Rubato may be described in several ways.

1. Any temporary retardation or acceleration is *rubato*.

2. Any negative grammatical accentuation (for example, syncopation), by which the time becomes robbed of its regular accents, is a *rubato*.

3. That capricious and disorderly mode of performance by which some notes are protracted beyond their proper duration and others curtailed, without, however, changing the aggregate duration of each measure, is a *rubato*.

The first of these three definitions requires no further observation.

The second, likewise, has been fully explained already, under Negative Grammatical Accents.

But the last mode, which is, in fact, the real *rubato*, as it is usually understood, will receive particular notice.

This latter mode of performance is the *rubato* of Chopin ; very beautiful and artistic when in its proper place and limitation, but very ugly and pernicious when out of place, or exaggerated.

It may be executed in two ways :

1. Both hands in sympathy with each other, *i. e.*, both hands accelerating or retarding together.

2. Or, the two hands not in sympathy, *i. e.*, the accompanying hand keeping strict time, while the other hand alone is playing *rubato*.

The latter way is the more beautiful of the two, and is the truly artistic *rubato*.

Chopin's often reiterated counsel to his pupils was substantially this : "Let ycur accompanying hand be your conductor, and let it keep time, even while your other hand plays *rubato.*"

Acting upon his own advice, Chopin was always a very good time-keeper ; and, in spite of using the greatest tact-freedom and taking the widest *rubato* liberties, his tact-transgressions never overstepped the limit of moderation or offensively interrupted the general tempo.   It is, there-fore, all the more to be regretted, that a large number of his admirers and imitators, forgetting, or perhaps unaware of these well-known traditions, imagine they are portraying the style and personality of the master, by spasmodically changing the gait of movement, at any moment, generally an uncalled-for one.   They thus misrepresent and caricature the very thing about which Chopin was most particular, viz. :

Tact-freedom within strictness ;
Tact-strictness within freedom.

There are musicians, who, believing absolute strictness to be an essen-tial quality, rarely indulge in a *ritardando* or *accelerando*; while others, fancying strictness to be equivalent to stiffness, hardly play in time at all.

Of these two extreme classes of performers, the first is not quite so objectionable as the second ; because who would not rather behold the straight-laced, rigid marching of a well-disciplined soldier, than the un-steady, vacillating gait of a musical rhapsodist, intoxicated by conceit or ignorance.

The former, the realist, though he cannot interest, is, nevertheless, a musician ; whereas the latter, the idealist, exasperates the listener, and is, in reference to time-keeping, simply a nuisance.

Without discussing such extreme cases, which should both be avoided, let us remember that the proper course to be pursued, in this respect (as in everything else pertaining to musical art), is to keep a *juste milieu*— the golden mean—between exaggeration and tameness.

Accepting this course as the only proper one, we find the surest and best safeguard against overdoing, in either direction, in Chopin's advice to his pupils, as already quoted.   In fact, we cannot overrate the importance of, or pay too much attention to, the principle of Chopin :

"*One hand should be kept in time, while the other hand retards or accelerates.*"

Now, it may be said that this is impossible.   But such is, by no means, the case.   Listen, in Italian opera, to a first-class singer, and notice how steadily the orchestral accompaniment proceeds, while the soloist retards and accelerates, at almost every moment.

It is just this steadiness and general not-giving-way of the accompaniment which the soloist needs and desires, expecting only from the conductor that he will follow, or either wait for him, at the *tenuto* or *fermate* points. Just so should the pianist keep time, and yet be free in time.

How well Thalberg understood the art of singing on the pianoforte, those who heard him can bear witness. And how little the majority of modern pianists know of it, is shown by the unsteady way in which they play accompaniments.

When Thalberg played a melody, it stood out in bold dynamic relief; not because he pounded, but because he kept the accompaniment duly subdued. And when he accelerated, retarded, or embellished his melody, the accompaniment proceeded with steady, unwavering precision, unaffected by the emotion displayed in the solo parts.

This method, far from being stiff or rigid, is not only rational and musical, but beautiful and highly artistic; never provoking and exasperating, as out-of-time playing with both hands, but always gratifying, attractive, and possessing a peculiar charm, which would be entirely lost, if the accompaniment were dependent on the melody, instead of independent of it.

This refers, of course, chiefly to homophonous music, and, particularly, to that kind of modern music which has a distinctly characteristic rhythm, such as dances and all descriptive modern pianoforte compositions.

Rhythm, being the real life of music, must be imperatively preserved, and not mutilated by fanciful or sentimental changes, at variance with the general character of a composition.

As the idea of a composition lies chiefly in its character, and the character is depicted in the rhythm, to mutilate the rhythm would be defacing the idea.

What is a waltz, a polonaise, a barcarole, or a lullaby, without the appropriate rhythm essential to each? And though, it may be argued, a waltz, a mazurka, a polonaise of Chopin, for example, is not really a dance, but a poetized dance-form ; yet, it may be answered, the rhythm must, nevertheless, be kept up, or the idea becomes a travesty and a farce, instead of being a poetical portraiture.

I remember reading somewhere, I think in Spohr's auto-biography, that, at an evening-party, Hummel, the pianist, was coaxed by some young ladies into playing a waltz, for them to dance to. Hummel being in one room, while the young folks were dancing in another, kept on playing, and, at the same time, conversing for nearly an hour; and, though diversifying his musical subjects in every imaginable way, letting even a little fugue creep in, yet he never relaxed or changed his time or tempo, and kept the merry feet a-going, until the young ladies came in a body to thank him, and crown him with an improvised wreath made with the flowers of their bouquets.

Now, although I do not intend to cite Hummel as a model as regards poetical interpretation, yet I mean to say that to play a waltz in waltz-tempo could certainly not impair the poetry of either the composition or the performance; while it is simply absurd to imagine that playing out of time, with the impression of its being *rubato*, could produce a more poetical effect.

Let the student try an experiment with a dance, choosing a waltz—the most pensive, melancholy, undancelike one. Let him play it, first, in the usual lackadaisical manner of sentimentalists, *i. e.*, placing sentiment above the character of the composition; and then play the waltz, again, in the character of a waltz, *i. e.*, keeping time with the accompaniment.

Comparing the effect, or better, judging the effect by the impression which each of these modes of rendering has upon competent listeners, the verdict, as to which is the most pleasing and acceptable, is scarcely to be doubted, and should be convincing.

A waltz must be a waltz, however opposed the sentiment of its music may be to its rhythm. Whatever *rubato* liberties may be taken with the melody, the rhythm (time) must be kept up, at least, in the accompaniment. What holds good in the case of a waltz is equally exigent in any other piece, in which the character is portrayed by the rhythm, such as: marches, mazurkas, polonaises, barcaroles, lullabies, serenades, etc., including even nocturnes, romances, and songs without words; in fact, every style of modern composition.

There is, perhaps, no one of the great pianoforte composers, whose individuality is better adapted to *rubato*, or whose creations more require the use of it, than Chopin; and among Chopin's works there is probably no class of composition more susceptible of *rubato*, than his mazurkas. In these, one may find perhaps the strongest illustration of his personality, in reference to *rubato* liberties.

If the student will try these mazurkas, or merely the earlier ones (Op. 6 and 7), and can succeed in playing them, each hand independently, the one in time, the other *rubato*, he will then understand what an artistic *rubato* signifies, and that its first condition is to guard against sacrificing the character of the piece for the sake of sentiment.

Character is the internal life of a piece, engendered by the composer; sentiment is the external impression, given to the work by the interpreter. Character is an intrinsic, positive part of a composition; sentiment, an extrinsic, personal matter only.

Character is innate, steady, precise; and, inasmuch as it is wholly expressed by the rhythm, more particularly by the time and tempo, the rendering of a piece can only be true to the character, if the time and tempo are generally upheld.

Sentiment, on the other hand, is extraneous, unsteady, varied; and, though it may be appropriate and true, yet it is frequently inappropriate and false.

It is, therefore, necessary to keep the sentiment under control, and to always maintain the character. In fact, sentiment should never be allowed to assume a prominence over, or be detrimental to, the character of a composition.

THE END.